Cook it Slow, Cook it Fast

More Than 150 Easy Recipes for Your Slow Cooker and Pressure Cooker

Chief Food Officer: Howard Rosenthal
Chief Executive Officer: Steve Ginsburg
Test Kitchen Director: Patty Rosenthal
Kitchen Assistant: Dave DiCarlo
Editor: Jodi Flayman
Editorial Team: Carol Ginsburg, Jaime Gross, Amy Magro, Merly Mesa, Michael Plontz, Rebecca Rubin
Photography: Kelly Rusin
Post Production: Hal Silverman of Hal Silverman Studio
Book Design: Lorraine Dan
Cover Concept & Graphic Elements: Rachel Johnson
Founder: Art Ginsburg

Inquiries should be addressed to:
Cogin, Inc.
1770 NW 64 Street, Suite 500
Fort Lauderdale, FL 33309

Library of Congress Cataloging-in-Publication Data
Mr. Food Test Kitchen
Mr. Food Test Kitchen Cook it Slow, Cook it Fast/ Mr. Food

ISBN 978-0-9911934-2-4
1. Cookery. 2. Quick and Easy. I. Title: Mr. Food Test Kitchen Cook it Slow, Cook it Fast. II. Title.

Printed in the United States of America
First Edition

www.MrFood.com

Contents

Introduction

Yes, we'll admit it. Before we started working on this cookbook, none of us in the Test Kitchen had a PhD in cooking in a slow cooker or pressure cooker. Sure, we knew the basics, and had dabbled over the years in cooking the famous corned beef and cabbage on St. Patrick's Day, or the same mac & cheese that everyone else was making, but that was about it! So, after months of research, followed by a year of testing and retesting, we finally mastered the art of slow cooking and pressure cooking, and we're excited to share it all with you!

Besides the mouthwatering recipes, we think one of the best parts of this book is that it's full of all the tips and tricks that we discovered along the way! We wanted to present it to you in an easy-to-read and easy-to-understand fashion, without all the overwhelming, fancy-schmancy terminology. You can feel confident about knowing that our recipes will deliver the results you expect from the Mr. Food Test Kitchen.

Most people who own a pressure cooker also own a slow cooker, which is why we combined these two, almost totally opposite styles of cooking into one book! Yep, you guys asked for a book like this, and we delivered! After all, whether you "cook it slow" or "cook it fast" the goal is the same – to get great tasting results that are easy.

So, what makes this book stand out from the many other cookbooks that are out there? This cookbook wasn't developed just for one brand of slow cooker or pressure cooker. Our goal was to create a book that you could enjoy whether you have a top-of-the-line model, the kind with all the bells and whistles, or a basic one that still delivers the results you want.

So, whether you want to cook it slow or cook it fast, you'll be armed with over 150 quick and easy recipes that will deliver great taste, time after time. It's like having two books in one!

Ok, enough of all this jibber-jabber, it's time to get cooking and start enjoying lots of...
"OOH IT'S SO GOOD!!®"

Before preparing any of these recipes, please make sure you do one thing: *Read the manual and the safety instructions that came with your slow cooker or pressure cooker. Although we make every effort to ensure that you have a safe and fun experience with your slow or pressure cooker, each model is slightly different and your manual will contain important information that is specific to your model.*

Slow Cooking 101

So, you bought this book or you got it as a gift, and you're not too sure about the whole slow cooker thing that everyone seems to be all excited about. Well, we could tell you about the many benefits we discovered while we tested and tasted recipe after recipe. Or we could tell you how moist and juicy recipes cooked in a slow cooker are... or that you can just put everything in and let the slow cooker do all the work while you do your thing, and on and on. But we feel the best way to truly appreciate the benefits of slow cooking is for you to actually make a recipe or two from the book and to experience the benefits firsthand. So, after you try a few recipes and discover how convenient it is to come home to a tasty, hot, and hearty dinner, you'll know why we and hundreds of thousands of others, are so passionate about our slow cookers. As they say: seeing is believing.

The Basic Principle:

Think of a slow cooker as an electric pot that cooks over a very low heat. There are four main components: the outer casing, the inner cooking insert /crock, the lid, and the control panel.

Let's check out the parts:

- **Outer casing:** This is a metal vessel which holds the cooking insert that contains low-wattage heating coils that are completely encased in it.
- **Cooking Insert/Crock:** It is made from either glazed ceramic or cast aluminum. It fit inside the casing. In most models, you can remove the cooking insert from the casing.
- **Lid:** The lid is almost always made of tempered glass and is dome- shaped. It usually has a silicon gasket or metal rim that creates a snug fit to the cooking vessel.
- **Control panel:** This typically has 3 settings: OFF, LOW, and HIGH. You'll find some that also have additional settings that include: WARM, SIMMER, BROWN, and SEAR.

Slow cookers use what is known as indirect heat. The slow cooking comes from the fact that it cooks at a low temperature for a longer period of time compared to traditional cooking methods.

What makes slow cooking so effective is that as the food cooks, it releases moisture which is trapped inside the covered cooking insert. This condensation creates a seal between the lid and the crock, which adds moisture to the food and helps the cooking process. That's why it's important to always cook with the lid on.

Hints and Tips for Using Slow Cookers:

Size Matters: When it comes to cooking in a slow cooker, size matters, just like it does when we're selecting the proper size pot. In all our recipes, we give a recommended size of slow cooker to use.

For example, we may suggest a "5-quart or larger slow cooker". That means in our testing, we determined that a 5-quart size allowed the recipe to cook properly and the cooking insert was full enough, but not too full. The rule of thumb is the insert should be about half to three-quarters full. But since it would not be practical to have so many different size slow cookers, we offer you the option of cooking most dishes, based on our example, in a 5-quart or larger slow cooker.

Sure there are exceptions, but that's a good rule of thumb. We do want to emphasize that these are guidelines and you should always follow the information given in the manual that comes with your slow cooker. One exception to this would be recipes that need a specific-sized slow cooker. A good example of this is when baking a cake in your slow cooker. If the slow cooker is too big, the cake will be too thin and will probably dry out based on the suggested cooking time. If it's too small, it most likely will not cook all the way through in the recommended time.

Also, many of the appetizers, usually dips, call for a specific range of size. An example would be "3- to 4-quart." Again, if the cooking insert is too large, it most likely will not cook properly for the small amount that is being cooked.

Digital vs. Manual Controls: Just like with most appliances, you'll find many variables when it comes to the bells and whistles, as you shop between brands and price points. Usually you'll find the manual (non-digital) slow cookers less expensive than the ones with the digital or fancy electronic controls. The digital models often allow you the ability to set a starting time, will automatically switch to a "Keep Warm" setting once cooking is complete, and some even have preset times programmed in so you can select a type of food and it will select a time based on that. Some of the higher priced slow cookers, or as they are often called, "multi-cookers," have a setting that allows you to "brown" (meats and veggies, for example) before the long cooking. They also have a setting that allows you to simmer or reduce sauces after the long cooking part of the recipe is complete.

Although these features are nice, only you will know how important these features are to you, so make sure you check out all your options carefully. That way you'll get the right make and model to suit your cooking style and budget.

What Is A Sling and How Do You Make One?: Since most slow cookers are rather deep compared to typical bakeware or cookware, it may be a bit more challenging to remove certain cooked items from the cooking insert. The solution to this is to make a sling that sits under the food before it's cooked and can be easily lifted out, along with the food, after it's cooked. This technique sure is handy when you want to remove a meatloaf or cake from the insert.

To make a sling, cut a piece of aluminum foil so it's about 18" long. Then fold it lengthwise over and over until you end up with a 2-inch wide strip of foil. Place this in the slow cooker as shown. Make sure the ends do not interfere with the food being cooked or the secure fit of the lid.

To Brown Or Not To Brown: The great debate over the need to brown meats or not has been around as long as the slow cooker. Unlike traditional cooking methods in the oven, the broiler, or on the stove top, most meats will not brown in a slow cooker. We discovered during our testing that it is not usually a necessity to brown, except when the meat is ground beef or ground turkey, for example. The purpose of doing that is to ensure the meat cooks through and is crumbled. If you don't brown ground meat as suggested, your chili will turn out more like meatloaf.

When it comes to roasts and other larger cuts of meats, since we eat with our eyes, you can always rub a little soy sauce or browning and seasoning sauce on your meat before putting it in your slow cooker. A little goes a long way. Think of it like giving your recipe a rub-on tan! If you do want to sear your roast, (all that means is to brown it in a hot pan) please feel free to do so.

Cooking In Another Pan: Think of your slow cooker as a mini oven that cooks nice and slow, providing a moist environment. After lots of testing, we discovered that many recipes such as banana bread, meatloaf, and many others are great when cooked in a slow cooker. But rather than putting the batter or the meat mixture directly in the cooking insert, we discovered that we can place it in a baking dish or loaf pan and then place that into the cooking insert to cook. See page 180 and 182 for examples of this. (Just make sure it fits in your slow cooker before using it.)

Keep A Lid On It: In order to maintain the proper cooking temperature and moisture level in your slow cooker, make sure you always cook with the lid on. Of course, like every rule there are always a few exceptions, but unless a recipe specifically calls out to go topless, or to remove the lid for one reason or another, keep the lid on.

Herbs – Fresh or Dried: There are a few tips you should remember when it comes to herbs. Dried herbs work well during the low and slow cooking process. Since the inside of your cooker is so moist, they rehydrate and add lots of flavor. And although we are big fans of fresh herbs, it's important to know that they will often turn dark in color during the long cooking process. Our suggestion would be to add fresh herbs during the last 15 minutes or so of cooking if you want them to maintain their bright color.

Rotating the Crock Means Even Cooking: You may find, depending on the brand of slow cooker you have, that one side of your slow cooker is hotter than the other. A way to reduce uneven cooking or baking is to remove the cooking insert halfway through the cooking process, and rotate it 180°. It will be hot so use pot holders. In most cases, the side opposite the control panel is the hottest side. This is usually more important when cooking a casserole or baking a cake than it is when cooking a roast.

Darn It, I Forgot To Take The Meat Out Of The Freezer!: Yes, it happens to all of us. We forget to thaw the chicken or roast we need for dinner tonight. If so, don't sweat it. Unless our recipes specifically call for meats that are fresh and not frozen at the time of cooking, you can usually adapt recipes to use frozen meats. When doing so, on most occasions you will need to add an additional 20 to 25% to the cooking time. This is only a rule of thumb. Always make sure you check for proper recommended doneness with an instant-read thermometer.

Don't Forget About Your Slow Cooker: We know this may sound crazy, but it is important to remember to put away any leftovers as soon as possible. Because slow cookers are so convenient, it's easy to forget the basic rules of food safety. Always make sure food is kept at a safe temperature.

The Paper Towel Trick: Since you will see that your slow cooker is far more versatile than a tool to simply cook soups and stews, at times you will find the condensation that builds up on the inside of the lid will drip onto whatever you are making and leave unwanted watermarks or a soggy topping. For example, if you're baking a cake, the water droplets will fall onto the top of the cake and leave little divots and water marks. This can be prevented by placing a couple of layers of paper towels over the top of the insert. It will stay in place once you put the lid on. It is important to make sure the paper towel is pulled tight, so it sits above the food that you're cooking and doesn't touch it.

Pressure Cooking 101

In our opinion, the pressure cooker should be called the fast cooker. If you want a lot of flavor in a little time, then you're going to love your pressure cooker. And if you're hesitant to use one because of safety concerns, don't worry, because today's pressure cookers have come a long way.

What do you say we help you explore the ins-and-outs of how to make the most of your pressure cooker, so you end up with more time to do what you want, have less dirty dishes, and of course, you'll get to enjoy lots more ... OOH IT'S SO GOOD!!®

The Basic Principles:

A pressure cooker is a pot with a locking lid that has a valve which regulates the pressure inside. As the pot heats up, the liquid inside forms steam, which increases the pressure. This high pressure and the steam that is created and locked inside, have two major effects. One is that it raises the temperature inside the pot. The other is that the high pressure forces moisture into whatever you are cooking, super quickly, since this environment minimizes evaporation. These elements help speed up the cooking process while keeping whatever you are cooking very flavorful and juicy.

Another big benefit is that all the flavors blend together so much better than with traditional cooking methods. So, say good-bye to boring and hello to lots of long-cooking flavor in a short time.

Different Styles of Pressure Cooking:

When it comes to options of pressure cooking, there are lots of choices. First thing to know is there are three basic types of pressure cookers: electric, stovetop and microwave. Although the principle is the same in all three methods, we feel there are pros and cons to each of them.

- **Electric:** Recently, we have seen a huge increase in the popularity of electric pressure cookers. This popularity is based on the fact that they are more automated than the stove top versions. They often have pre-set as well as auto on and off features to make them more foolproof. Some models will even switch to a keep-warm mode once the timer goes off.

  The down side we found with these is that unless you have a "multi-cooker" type model, it can be more challenging to "brown" meats and "simmer" sauces in the same pan. Also, due to their energy efficient design, electric pressure cookers take much longer to cool down and to naturally release pressure. This can result in your recipes becoming overcooked.

- **Stove Top:** We tested these recipes in both a stove top model and an electric model. The benefits we found in the stove top models are easier regulation of temperature and the ability to easily "brown" meats and "simmer" sauces.

  The down side is that there is no liner pan when cooking in a stove top version like there is with electric models, so you do need to be careful that you don't scorch the bottom of the pot. Also, with stove top models, you need to set a timer as they are not automatic.

- **Microwave:** The new option that we are seeing more and more of, is a pressure cooker that goes in the microwave. Although we only tested this in a handful of our recipes, we found that it delivered consistent results to the electric and stove top models. Based on your microwave, your will need to adjust cooking time on recipes as appropriate.

  The down side we found was that the pressure cooker was a bit smaller in order to fit in most microwaves. You can always cut recipes in half, if necessary.

Let's check out the parts:

- **Cooking Pot:** This looks similar to any other basic stainless steel pot and will vary in size. They usually range from 5 to 8 quart. We prefer ones that have wider bottoms which allow more surface area to sauté or to spread out what is being cooked. Electric pressure cookers have a non-stick insert that fits inside a casing which houses the heating elements.

- **Locking Lid:** Whether you have a stove top or electric pressure cooker, the lid is very different from any other lid you have in your kitchen. It actually locks onto the pot creating an airtight seal, and has regulators that control the amount of pressure that builds up in your pot. See below for more detail.

- **Handle:** Just like with your regular pot and pans, these vary in size, shape, and material. Make sure you select one that feels good to you and that will provide you the support you need. On stove top models, the handles are also part of the locking system and often have indicators that help you align the pot with the lid.

- **Pressure Safety Lock:** Every manufacturer seems to have their own design for this, but the principle is always the same. It lets you know when the lid is on correctly and is in the lock position.

- **Pressure Indicator:** These vary from model to model. The basic role these play is to let you know when the pot is under pressure. Some are little pins that "pop up," others have color indicators, and so on.

- **Pressure Release Valve:** Again, these will vary from one model to another. Most often though, there is an adjustable valve that will allow you to manually release pressure/steam after you are done cooking. It will be marked to indicate something like: open/closed or pressure/release.

- **Safety Vents:** These are what make today's pressure cookers so much safer than the older models. They allow pressure/steam to release in the event that the main valves become clogged with food or for any another reason.

Pressure Cooking Lingo:

Securely lock lid: In all our recipes, you will find that we say to "securely lock lid". To do so, you'll need to follow the manufacturer's instructions on how to properly do this for your particular model. Typically, you line up a marker on the pot with a marker on the lid, then twist until the lid and pot are lined up. Some have an indicator, while others have a lock button. It's easy once you do it a few times.

Bring to full pressure: Once you have the lid in place, heat the pot on medium-high until it comes up to pressure. You'll be able to tell when it comes to pressure by a good amount of steam coming out of the vents. This will take anywhere from 5 to 15 minutes, depending upon how full the pot is and how much liquid you use. If your pot has an old fashioned jiggler on top, when it starts to jiggle and steam starts to release, it's at full pressure. Many cookers allow you to select high or low pressure.

Reduce heat just enough to maintain pressure: Once you reach the pressure, turn down the stove immediately and set a timer for whatever time the recipe calls for. For most stove tops, turning it down to medium-low is just right to maintain the proper pressure. You're still going to see some steam coming out of the pressure release valve -- that's normal. If you're cooking on an electric stove, where the burners take a bit of time to cool down, you might consider moving your pressure cooker from the burner you brought it up to pressure on, to another burner with lower heat so it quickly maintains the proper pressure and will not scorch the pot.

Maintain pressure for XX minutes: This is what we refer to as the cooking time. Unlike other methods of cooking, since this cooks so fast, make sure you set a timer if you are using a stove top pressure cooker. The electric ones have built-in timers.

Perform a quick release: The quick method involves relieving the pressure manually, by either opening the pressure release valve or running the pot under cold running water. Most of today's pressure cookers come with a valve that allows you to release the pressure by simply opening the valve. When doing this, always be careful and direct the hot steam away from your body and face. If you choose to run the pot under cold water, which cools it down quickly, try to avoid running the water over the valves.

Perform a natural release: The natural method lets the steam dissipate on its own and takes about 10-15 minutes. The fuller the pot, the longer it takes. Be sure to follow the recipe instructions to the letter, because, if the steam releases gradually, it will continue to cook the food, and might cause overcooking. If you have an electric pressure cooker, you may want to perform a quick release after 15 minutes or so to ensure your food does not overcook. These take considerably longer to release pressure naturally, because they retain the heat longer.

Let us share with you a few things that we discovered as we spent some quality time with our pressure cookers:

Add the Right Amount of Liquid: Without liquid, your food won't cook properly in a pressure cooker. Although the liquid is usually water, broth, or some type of soup, canned tomatoes and other juicy foods also count as a liquid. The rule of thumb is that you need at least 1 cup of liquid to create the steam needed. If you don't have enough liquid, the pan will probably burn on the bottom and your recipe will be ruined. For best results, follow the recipe exactly.

Trivets, Steamer Baskets, Steamer Inserts, and Foil Collars: There are times when you're going to want to elevate the food or the dish so that it is above the liquid in the pressure cooker. This allows larger cuts of meat from sitting directly on the bottom of the pot or casserole dishes from sitting in water while they cook. Using the rack method will reduce the chances of scorching. To do so, you can use a metal trivet (without plastic feet), a steamer basket, or steamer insert (that often comes with your pressure cooker).

If you don't have any of these, you can always create a foil collar to accomplish this. And because you're creating the collar yourself, you can make it any size you want. For instance, you can make mini rings for ramekins or one large ring to elevate a casserole dish. All you have to do is cut an 18-inch piece of foil, bunch it up like a rope, and create a circle the size you need.

A Sling Comes in Very Handy: Slings come in handy when you want to lower a baking dish into a pressure cooker or remove it without making a mess. All you do is cut an 18-inch piece of foil and fold it over and over until you end up with a 2-inch strip of foil. Then carefully place it under your baking dish that fits into your pressure cooker, and gently lower it into the bottom of the pot. Fold over the excess foil so it doesn't interfere with the cooking or the securing of the pressurized lid. When the cooking is complete, you can carefully use the sling to remove the cooked dish safely.

Order of Ingredients Sometimes Matters: If we specify the order in which to add ingredients, it's for a reason. For example: thicker tomato products such as spaghetti sauce, ketchup, and salsa should be added last, and should not be stirred together with other ingredients. This will prevent the sugars in them from scorching while cooking. The same is true for any sugar or thick sauces.

Play it Safe: When you are releasing steam, always make sure to keep your hands and face away from the release valve. Also, always make sure you keep it turned away from you, as the steam will be hot and liquids can sputter. When removing the lid, even though the pressure will be reduced to a point that allows you to open the pot, there will still be a fair amount of steam in the pot. So make sure you tilt the lid to avoid getting a blast of steam in your face.

Cooking in a Crock: To have more options, on occasion, you can cook select recipes in oven-safe baking dishes. We have made bread puddings pages 21 and 194 using this method. When doing this, always make sure the dish is oven-safe and that you leave at least ½-inch all around the dish so that the steam in the pressure cooker can circulate and it cooks evenly. Always make sure your dish fits inside your pressure cooker before you start to make your recipe. Also, we recommend always placing it on a steamer rack or collar (see above) so the dish is not sitting directly on the bottom of the pressure cooker. Don't fill these containers more than 2/3 full to allow for food expansion.

Don't Overfill: The rule of thumb is to never fill your pressure cooker more than 2/3 full, whether it's a stovetop model, electric, or for the microwave. The remaining space is needed to generate steam which allows the pressure to build.

Hints and Tips for Using Electric Pressure Cookers

Although there are many similarities between stove top pressure cookers and electric ones, there are a few techniques that are different. We want to point these out so you can have the same great results no matter what brand or type of pressure cooker you are using.

Setting the Timer for the Suggested Cooking Time:
Unlike a stove top pressure cooker where you have to manually reduce the heat to maintain pressure and then set a timer so you know when to turn it off, electric models, for the most part, are automated.

You just enter the number of minutes that the recipe suggests, after the lid is secure, and the pressure cooker will preheat, adjust the temperature to maintain the pressure, and then turn off after the set time is up. Please note that the time you set is the cooking time and does not include the time it takes to pre-heat your pressure cooker as the pressure builds up.

We did find some pressure cookers have minimum times that you can set them for. If the time the recipe suggests is shorter than what you can set your electric pressure cooker for, set the pressure cooker to the lowest time possible just to activate it, but then set a different timer. When the extra timer goes off, unplug your cooker and proceed as directed in the recipe.

Although many electric models have pre-set buttons, we did not feature them in the recipes as they have large variances between models and manufacturers. See your manual that comes with your pressure cooker for more info.

To Simmer Sauces:
If the recipe calls for the finished dish to simmer, so the sauce can thicken or reduce, you have a few options:

- If your electric pressure cooker has a "simmer" setting...hooray! That will make it easy. Just set it to simmer, with the lid off of course, and let it do its thing.
- No simmer feature, no problem. Once the pressure cooker automatically turns off, set the timer for a few more minutes as if you were about to cook in it like normal. Leave the lid off and let it simmer. Most likely the cooking temp will be higher, so keep an eye on it.
- The last option is to transfer your sauce or recipe to a regular pot and simmer it on your stove top like you would normally do. (Never put your pressure cooker insert directly on the stove top, though.)

Browning Meats or Sautéing In An Electric Pressure Cooker:
In a stove top pressure cooker, you can brown or sauté meats and such just like you would in your regular cookware. The only difference might be that since pressure cookers are made of stainless steel, make sure your pan is well heated before you start to brown or sauté.

If your electric pressure cooker has a "brown" or "sauté" setting, simply follow the instructions on the recipe as directed. Always make sure the lid is off when you're sautéing or browning. Please note, in most cases, electric pressure cookers do not get as hot as stove top models during the browning mode, so it most likely will take longer.

If your pressure cooker does not have these features, you have two choices.

- The first would be to brown or sauté in your everyday cookware, then transfer to the pressure cooker for the rest of the recipe.
- Another option would be to set your pressure cooker for a certain number of minutes, depending on what you are browning or sautéing, then place your food in the cooking insert. (Do not let your non-stick liner pre-heat.) Also, make sure you keep the lid off. Most likely your pressure cooker will turn off automatically after about 5 minutes, if it recognizes that no liquid is present.

Rise & Shine Favorites

Chocolate Lover's French Toast

Serves 6

- 6 thick slices egg bread, like challah
- ½ cup chocolate chips
- 6 eggs
- 3 cups half-and-half
- ⅔ cup sugar
- 2 teaspoons vanilla extract
- ¼ teaspoon salt

1. Coat a 5-quart or larger oval slow cooker with cooking spray.
2. Place 2 slices of bread on bottom of slow cooker. Sprinkle with half the chocolate chips. Top with 2 more bread slices, the remaining chocolate chips, and the remaining slices of bread.
3. In a bowl, beat eggs. Whisk in half-and-half, sugar, vanilla, and salt. Pour mixture over bread layers. Gently press bread into liquid making sure it's covered. Let sit 10 minutes, allowing the bread to absorb most of the liquid.
4. Cover and cook on HIGH 3 hours, or until center is set.

Fancy This Up:

Watch everyone come running to the breakfast table once they get a whiff of this baking! Once they see it topped with some powdered sugar, or maybe with some whipped cream and a drizzle of chocolate sauce, just watch how fast their sleepy eyes open wide.

Farmer's Ham & Cheese Quiche

Serves 4

- 2 eggs
- 1 cup half-and-half
- 1 cup shredded Cheddar cheese
- 1 cup shredded Swiss cheese
- ½ cup pancake and baking mix
- 1 teaspoon onion powder
- ½ teaspoon salt
- ¼ teaspoon black pepper
- 2 cups frozen chopped broccoli, thawed
- ½ cup diced ham

1. Coat a 4-quart or larger slow cooker with cooking spray.
2. In a large bowl, beat the eggs and half-and-half together until well combined. Add remaining ingredients and stir. Pour into slow cooker.
3. Cover and cook on LOW 3-½ to 4 hours or on HIGH 2-½ to 3 hours, or until center is set.

Serving Suggestion:
If you want to serve this bright and early, why not make the batter the night before? That way in the morning all ya have to do is pour it in, turn it on, and let it cook while everyone slowly wakes up.

Layered Biscuit Bake

SLOW COOKER

Serves 8

- 1 (16.3-ounce) package refrigerated buttermilk biscuits (8 biscuits)
- 12 eggs
- ¼ cup milk
- 2 scallions, sliced
- 1 teaspoon salt
- ½ teaspoon black pepper
- 1-¼ cups (5 ounces) shredded Cheddar cheese, divided
- ¾ cup bacon bits

1. Coat a 4-quart or larger slow cooker with cooking spray. Cut each biscuit into 6 pieces.
2. In a large bowl, whisk together the eggs, milk, scallions, salt, and pepper until well mixed. Stir 1 cup of cheese and the bacon bits into egg mixture. Add biscuit pieces and toss to coat evenly. Pour mixture into slow cooker.
3. Cook on HIGH 1-½ to 1-¾ hours, or until center is set. Sprinkle remaining cheese over top and cook 10 to 15 additional minutes, or until cheese is melted. Serve immediately.

Food for Thought:
Even though all the ingredients get mixed together, they separate into layers as it bakes. It's like a little kitchen miracle!

Greek Frittata

Serves 4

- ¼ cup olive oil
- 1 (32-ounce) package frozen potato tots
- 1 dozen eggs
- 1 (10-ounce) package frozen chopped spinach, thawed and squeezed dry
- 1 cup (4-ounces) crumbled feta cheese
- 1 teaspoon dried oregano
- 1 teaspoon salt
- ½ teaspoon black pepper

1. Coat a 4-quart or larger slow cooker with cooking spray.
2. In a skillet over high heat, heat oil until hot. Add potato tots and cook 8 to 10 minutes, or until golden brown, stirring occasionally. Transfer to slow cooker.
3. Meanwhile, in a large bowl, whisk together eggs, spinach, cheese, oregano, salt and pepper until well mixed. Pour over potatoes.
4. Cover and cook on HIGH 1 to 1-¼ hours, or until set in the middle. Serve immediately.

Make sure you really use some elbow grease when you squeeze the water out of the spinach, 'cause soggy spinach leads to a soggy frittata. We wouldn't want that, would we?

Deli-Style Hash 'n' Eggs

Serves 6

- 1 stick butter, cut into pieces
- 1 cup diced onion
- 1 (32-ounce) package frozen diced hash brown potatoes, thawed
- 1 pound diced cooked corned beef
- ½ green bell pepper, diced
- ½ teaspoon salt
- ¼ teaspoon black pepper
- 6 eggs

1. Coat a 5-quart or larger oval slow cooker with cooking spray.
2. In a large bowl, combine butter, onion, hash browns, corned beef, bell pepper, salt, and pepper. Pour mixture into slow cooker and even off top.
3. Cover and cook on LOW about 3 hours or on HIGH 1-½ to 2 hours, or until hash is heated through.
4. Using the back of a spoon, make 6 shallow wells in hash. Crack an egg into each well.
5. Cover and cook on LOW about 25 minutes, or until eggs are just set. Serve immediately.

Pedro's Breakfast Potatoes

SLOW COOKER

Serves 8

- 20 links brown 'n' serve sausage, cut into bite-sized pieces
- 1 (32-ounce) package frozen diced hash brown potatoes
- 1 onion, chopped
- 1 red bell pepper, chopped
- 1 cup (4 ounces) shredded Mexican cheese blend
- 1 (7-ounce) can chopped green chilies, drained
- ½ stick (4 tablespoons) butter, melted
- 1 teaspoon cumin
- ½ teaspoon salt
- ¼ teaspoon black pepper
- ½ teaspoon paprika

1. Coat a 4-quart or larger slow cooker with cooking spray. Place all ingredients in slow cooker and mix until well combined.
2. Cover and cook on LOW 8 to 9 hours or on HIGH 4 to 4-½ hours, or until heated through. Stir half way through cooking time.

Serving Suggestion:
Serve these topped with some scrambled eggs, a bit of fresh salsa, and some chopped cilantro. Now that's good eatin'.

Cinnamon Apple Monkey Bread

Serves 12

- ¾ cup packed brown sugar
- ¾ cup granulated sugar
- 1 tablespoon cinnamon
- 4 (7-½-ounce) cans refrigerated biscuits (10 biscuits each)
- 1-½ cups diced, peeled apples
- ½ cup chopped walnuts
- 1 stick butter, melted
- ⅓ cup apple juice
- 1 teaspoon vanilla extract

1. Coat a 4-quart or larger slow cooker with cooking spray.
2. In a small bowl, mix together brown sugar, granulated sugar, and cinnamon. Sprinkle 2 tablespoons of the mixture in the bottom of slow cooker. Set remaining mixture aside.
3. Cut each biscuit into 4 pieces and place in a large bowl along with apples, walnuts, and remaining sugar mixture. In a small bowl, mix together butter, apple juice, and vanilla; pour over biscuits and apples; toss gently to coat. Place in slow cooker.
4. Cover and cook on HIGH 2 to 2-½ hours, or until a knife inserted in center comes out clean. Turn off slow cooker and uncover; let cool 10 minutes. Run a knife around the edge to loosen from sides, then carefully invert onto a serving platter. Spoon any remaining topping onto bread. Serve warm.

Make sure you don't allow this to cool too much before flipping it. If you do, the caramel will set up and it will stick to the pan. Also, make sure you use pot holders as it'll be very hot.

Slow Cooker Eggs Benedict

Serves 4

- 4 English muffins, split, each half cut into 6 wedges
- 6 ounces Canadian bacon, cut into quarters
- 10 eggs
- ¼ cup milk
- 1 teaspoon salt
- ¼ teaspoon black pepper
- 1 (1.25-ounce) package hollandaise sauce mix, prepared according to package directions, warmed

1. Coat a 3- to 4-quart slow cooker with cooking spray.
2. Place English muffin wedges in slow cooker and top with Canadian bacon.
3. In a bowl, whisk eggs, milk, salt, and pepper; evenly pour over bacon.
4. Cover and cook on HIGH 1-¾ to 2 hours, or until center is set. Scoop egg mixture onto plates and top each with hollandaise sauce. Serve immediately.

Lighten This Up:

You can use deli smoked turkey instead of the Candian bacon, whole wheat English muffins and refrigerated liquid egg.

Blueberry Breakfast Bread Pudding

Serves 6

- 1 (8-ounce) package cream cheese, softened
- 8 large eggs
- 2 cups half-and-half
- 1 cup strawberry preserves
- 1 teaspoon vanilla extract
- 14 to 16 slices hearty white bread, cut into 1-inch cubes (about 10 cups)
- 2 cups fresh or frozen blueberries
- 2 tablespoons confectioners' sugar

1. Coat a 5-quart or larger slow cooker with cooking spray.
2. In a large bowl with an electric mixer, beat cream cheese until smooth. Add eggs, a couple at a time, beating well after each addition. Add half-and-half, strawberry preserves, and vanilla; mix until smooth. Gently add in bread cubes and blueberries and stir until evenly coated. Pour into slow cooker.
3. Cover and cook on HIGH 3 hours, or until center is set. Sprinkle with confectioners' sugar and serve immediately.

Serving Suggestion:
Sure this is good just like this, but why not go all out and drizzle this with some blueberry syrup? Yup, you should be able to find that right next to the pancake syrup in your market. Yummy!

Cinnamon Roll Coffee Cake

SLOW COOKER

Serves 6

- 2 cups pancake and baking mix
- 1 cup milk
- ½ cup sour cream
- 2 eggs
- ¾ cup sugar, divided
- 1 teaspoon vanilla extract
- 1 teaspoon cinnamon
- ½ cup chopped walnuts, divided
- 2 tablespoons butter, melted

1. Coat a 3-quart or larger slow cooker with cooking spray.
2. In a large bowl, combine baking mix, milk, sour cream, eggs, ½ cup sugar, and the vanilla and stir until smooth. Pour into slow cooker.
3. In a bowl, mix together remaining sugar, the cinnamon, ¼ cup walnuts, and the butter. Sprinkle mixture over batter. With a butter knife, gently swirl the topping into the batter to create a marbled effect. Sprinkle with remaining walnuts.
4. Cover and cook on HIGH 1-¼ to 1-½ hours, or until center is set.

Did You Know?

Cakes cooked in the slow cooker tend to be more moist than traditional ones baked in the oven, since the steam inside the slow cooker gets trapped in it as it bakes. See, ya learn something new every day!

Apple Cinnamon Oatmeal

Serves 6

- 2 apples, peeled, cored, and chopped
- 1-½ cups water
- 1-½ cups fat-free milk
- 1 cup steel-cut oats
- ½ cup chopped walnuts
- ½ cup dried cranberries
- 2 tablespoons maple syrup
- 2 tablespoons butter, cut into pieces
- ½ teaspoon cinnamon
- ¼ teaspoon salt

1. Coat a 4-quart or larger slow cooker with cooking spray.
2. Place all ingredients in slow cooker. Stir well, cover, and cook on HIGH 2 hours on LOW 4 hours, or until cooked to desired consistency, adding more water if needed.

Food for Thought:
If ya throw this together (on HIGH) before you have your first cup of coffee, it'll ready by the time the kids are out of bed.

Our Favorite Granola

Makes 7 cups

- 5 cups rolled oats
- 1 cup raw, whole almonds
- ¾ cup honey
- ¼ cup canola oil
- 1 teaspoon vanilla extract
- ½ cup pumpkin seeds (pepitas)
- ½ cup dried cranberries
- ¼ cup unsweetened shredded coconut

1. In a 4-quart or larger slow cooker, combine oats, almonds, honey, oil, and vanilla. Leave uncovered, and cook on HIGH 1 hour, stirring every 20 to 30 minutes. Reduce heat to LOW and add pumpkin seeds, cranberries, and coconut. Continue to cook uncovered about 2 hours, stirring every 20 to 30 minutes, or until granola is completely dry and starts to brown.

2. Pour granola onto baking sheets to cool. Store in an airtight container.

Serving Suggestion:

Not only is this good mixed into your yogurt and cereal, but we discovered that if we keep a small container of it nearby at all times, it's a great healthy anytime snack.

Old-Fashioned Apple Butter

SLOW COOKER

Makes 6 cups

- 6 pounds apples, peeled, cored, and sliced into ½-inch slices
- 1 cup lightly packed light brown sugar
- 1 cup granulated sugar
- 1 tablespoon cinnamon
- ½ teaspoon nutmeg
- ¼ teaspoon cloves
- ¼ teaspoon salt
- 1 tablespoon vanilla extract

1. Place apples in a 5-quart or larger slow cooker.
2. In a bowl, combine brown sugar, granulated sugar, cinnamon, nutmeg, cloves, and salt. Sprinkle over apples and stir until well combined.
3. Cover and cook on LOW about 8 hours or on HIGH about 4 hours, or until apples are very soft, stirring occasionally. Uncover, stir in vanilla, and continue cooking uncovered about 1 hour.
4. In a blender, or using an immersion blender, puree the apples until smooth. Spoon mixture into a container, cover, and refrigerate up to 2 weeks.

Serving Suggestion:

This is called apple butter since you can use it like butter on your toast. This is also awesome on top of grilled chicken or pork. Once you try it you'll probably discover lots of other uses. (Maybe even eat spoonfuls of it right from the bowl!)

Waffles and Berry Sauce

Serves 8

- 1 (16-ounce) package frozen blackberries
- 1 (16-ounce) package frozen strawberries
- 1 (16-ounce) package frozen raspberries
- 1-½ cups granulated sugar
- ½ cup plus 4 tablespoons water, divided
- 1 teaspoon vanilla extract
- 1 tablespoon lemon zest
- 2 tablespoons cornstarch
- 8 frozen waffles

1. In a 5-quart or larger pressure cooker, combine berries, sugar and ½ cup water; mix well.
2. Securely lock lid and over high heat, bring to full pressure; reduce heat just enough to maintain pressure for 3 minutes. Perform a natural release. Remove lid and stir in vanilla and lemon zest.
3. In a small bowl, combine remaining water and cornstarch. Slowly whisk into berry mixture and simmer on low. Continue to heat over low heat, uncovered, until thickened.
4. Toast waffles and serve immediately topped with berry sauce. Let any remaining berry sauce cool and refrigerate until ready to use.

Food for Thought:

Using frozen berries makes this come together really quickly, as the berries go from freezer to slow cooker with no thawing. It also means you can make this year round.

If using an electric pressure cooker prepare as directed above except:

- In step 2 set timer for 3 minutes.
- In step 3 simmer according to manufacturer's directions for your model.

For more details about how to use an electric pressure cooker, see pages xv-xvi.

Cheesy Potato Breakfast Bowl

- 5 cups (2-inch) cubed potatoes
- 1 onion, cut into 1-inch chunks
- ½ cup water
- ½ cup milk
- 2 tablespoons butter
- ½ teaspoon salt
- ⅛ teaspoon black pepper
- 2 cups shredded sharp Cheddar cheese
- 4 ounces processed cheese (like Velveeta)
- ½ cup crumbled cooked bacon
- 6 eggs, fried

1. Coat a 5-quart or larger pressure cooker with cooking spray. Add potatoes, onion, water, milk, butter, salt, and pepper.
2. Securely lock lid and over high heat, bring to full pressure; reduce heat just enough to maintain pressure for 3 minutes. Perform a quick release.
3. Add both cheeses and gently stir until melted and creamy. Spoon into individual serving bowls, top each with a fried egg, and sprinkle with bacon.

Howard Says:

"Think of this as a breakfast version of mac & cheese, but instead of using pasta, we use potatoes. Yummy!"

If using an electric pressure cooker prepare as directed above except:

- In step 2, set timer for 3 minutes.

For more details about how to use an electric pressure cooker, *see pages xv-xvi.*

Tutti Frutti Oatmeal

Serves 4

- 1 cup steel cut oats
- 2 cups milk
- 2 cups water
- 1 tablespoon butter
- 2 tablespoons brown sugar
- ¼ cup chopped walnuts
- ½ cup raisins
- ¾ cup chopped dried apricots
- ¼ teaspoon salt

1. In a 4-quart or larger pressure cooker, combine all ingredients. Securely lock lid and over high heat, bring to full pressure; reduce heat just enough to maintain pressure for 10 minutes. Perform a natural release.

Did You Know?

Cooking dried fruits in the pressure cooker, like we did here, makes them really plump and super juicy.

If using an electric pressure cooker prepare as directed above except:

- In step 1, set timer for 10 minutes.

For more details about how to use an electric pressure cooker, see pages xv-xvi.

Donut Bread Pudding

PRESSURE COOKER

Serves 12

- 1 (14-ounce) can sweetened condensed milk
- ¾ cup milk
- 3 eggs, beaten
- 1 teaspoon vanilla extract
- 1 teaspoon cinnamon
- ⅛ teaspoon salt
- ¾ cup raisins
- 8 glazed donuts, cut into cubes

1. Make a foil sling and place in a 6-quart or larger pressure cooker, with foil ends hanging over sides. Pour 1 cup water into pressure cooker. Coat a 1-½-quart ovenproof container that fits into your pressure cooker with cooking spray.

2. In a large bowl, whisk together condensed milk, milk, eggs, vanilla, cinnamon, and salt. Stir in raisins and donut cubes. Pour mixture into prepared container and place in pressure cooker. Fold foil sling ends over container.

3. Securely lock lid and over high heat, bring to full pressure; reduce heat just enough to maintain pressure for 15 minutes. Perform a quick release. Remove lid and using pot holders, lift container using the sling.

Howard Says:

"This is the kind of recipe that if you're wondering how many calories it has, you don't really want to know! But if you're looking for a great breakfast sweet...this is it!"

If using an electric pressure cooker prepare as directed above except:

- In step 3 set timer for 15 minutes.

For more details about how to use an electric pressure cooker, see pages xv-xvi.

Mr. Food
TEST KITCHEN
"OOH IT'S SO GOOD!!"
Mr. Food
TEST KITCHEN

Dips, Nibbles & Munchies

Slow Cooker Lettuce Wraps

Serves 6

- 1-½ pounds ground turkey
- ½ cup chopped onion
- ¾ cup hoisin sauce, divided
- ½ cup soy sauce
- 3 cloves garlic, minced
- 1 teaspoon dried ginger
- 2 tablespoons brown sugar
- 1 tablespoon sesame oil
- 1 (8-ounce) can water chestnuts, drained, chopped
- 2 cups bean sprouts
- 12 Boston bibb lettuce leaves

1. In a large skillet over high heat, cook turkey and onion 5 to 7 minutes, or until no pink remains.
2. In a 5-quart or larger slow cooker, combine turkey mixture, ½ cup hoisin sauce, the soy sauce, garlic, ginger, brown sugar, sesame oil, and water chestnuts.
3. Cover and cook on LOW 3 hours. Before serving, stir in bean sprouts and give it a toss.
4. Evenly divide the mixture between the lettuce leaves, drizzle with remaining hoisin sauce, and serve.

Serving Suggestions:

We like to serve these with shredded carrots, scallions, and chopped peanuts. And, if you'd like, how about whipping up a quick dipping sauce for these by mixing together ½ cup soy sauce, 3 tablespoons each sesame oil and rice wine vinegar, and some sliced scallions? Just put it into individual bowls to avoid the dreaded double dipping.

Italian Party Dip

Makes about 4 cups

- 2 cups (8 ounces) shredded mozzarella cheese
- 1 (24-ounce) jar spaghetti sauce
- ½ cup chopped pepperoni
- ½ teaspoon garlic powder
- ½ teaspoon Italian seasoning
- 1 (2.25-ounce) can sliced black olives, drained

1. Spray a 3- to 4-quart slow cooker with cooking spray. Combine all ingredients in the slow cooker and stir.
2. Cook on HIGH 45 to 60 minutes. Stir until smooth. Reduce heat to LOW to keep warm while serving.

Sure you could make this on the stovetop, but how would you keep it warm to serve? That's why making it in a slow cooker makes so much sense! Oh, and try serving it with crispy breadsticks or chunks of Italian bread for dipping.

Unstuffed Stuffed Mushroom Dip

SLOW COOKER

Makes about 6 cups

- ½ pound hot ground pork sausage
- 2 teaspoons minced garlic
- 1 (10.5-ounce) can cream of mushroom soup
- 1 (6-ounce) box herbed stuffing mix
- ½ pound fresh mushrooms, diced
- ½ cup diced red pepper
- 1 (4-ounce) package goat cheese
- ¼ teaspoon Italian seasoning

1. In a large skillet over medium-high heat, cook sausage and garlic, stirring until the sausage crumbles and is no longer pink; drain.
2. Add sausage to a 3- to 4-quart slow cooker. Stir in remaining ingredients.
3. Cover and cook on LOW 2 hours. Keep on LOW when serving.

Serving Suggestion:

This has all the taste of stuffed mushrooms without all the work of stuffing them. Simply spread this on practically anything and get ready for some good nibbling.

The Easiest Spinach Artichoke Dip Ever

Makes about 3 cups

- 1 (10-ounce) package frozen chopped spinach, thawed, squeezed dry
- 1 (8-ounce) package cream cheese, softened
- 1 cup shredded Swiss cheese
- ½ cup grated Parmesan cheese
- ¼ cup mayonnaise
- 2 tablespoons fresh lemon juice
- ½ teaspoon garlic powder
- 1 (14-ounce) can artichoke hearts, drained, chopped
- 1 French bread, sliced

1. In a large bowl, combine spinach, cream cheese, Swiss cheese, Parmesan cheese, mayonnaise, lemon juice, and garlic powder; beat until well blended. Stir in artichokes, then spoon into a 2-½-quart slow cooker.

2. Cook on LOW for 1-½ hours, or until cheese is melted and mixture is heated through. Keep on LOW to serve hot, with French bread.

Good for You!

If you want to lighten things up, feel free to use the lower fat versions of cream cheese and Swiss cheese and it'll still be yummy. We also tested this with fat-free versions of the cheeses and discovered it's not the same, so avoid those this time.

Ooey Gooey Buffalo Chicken Dip

Makes about 4 cups

- 1 (8-ounce) package cream cheese, softened
- 1 cup refrigerated chunky blue cheese dressing
- ½ cup Buffalo wing sauce
- 2 cups shredded rotisserie chicken
- ½ cup chopped celery

1. In a 2-½- to 3-quart slow cooker, mix cream cheese, dressing, and wing sauce. Stir in chicken and cover.
2. Heat on LOW 1 hour, or until cheese is melted and dip is heated through. Stir in celery.
3. Keep on LOW to serve hot.

Serving Suggestion:

Make sure ya serve this with lots of pita chips & cut up veggies so you can dip to your heart's content. We've even spread this on slices of pizza to make ordinary pizza... extraordinary!

Scoopable Brie Dip

Makes about 2 cups

- 1 (8-½-ounce) brie wheel, unwrapped, cut into 1-inch cubes
- ¼ cup dried cranberries
- ¼ cup chopped pecans
- 1 tablespoon brown sugar
- 1 tablespoon water
- ½ teaspoon balsamic vinegar

1. Place the brie cubes in a 2-cup oven-safe baking dish that will fit in your slow cooker.
2. In a small bowl, combine remaining ingredients; pour over brie. Place the baking dish in the center of a 2-½ quart or larger slow cooker.
3. Cook on LOW 4 hours or on HIGH 2- to 2-½ hours, or until hot and melty. Serve immediately.

Based on when you want to serve this, feel free to adjust the heat setting. Oops...we almost forgot to mention that you're gonna want to serve this with wedges of apple and French bread slices to spread this on.

Cheesy Chicken Nacho Dip

Makes about 6 cups

- 1 (16-ounce) package prepared cheese product with jalapeño peppers, cut into cubes (we used Velveeta)
- 1 (15-ounce) can black beans, rinsed and drained
- 1 (9-ounce) package frozen Southwest-seasoned chicken breast strips, thawed and chopped
- 3/4 cup chunky salsa
- 1 cup refrigerated ranch sour cream dip
- 2 red bell peppers, chopped
- 1 (13-ounce) bag tortilla chips

1. In a 3-quart or larger slow cooker, mix together cheese, beans, chicken, and salsa.
2. Cover and cook on LOW 2-½ to 3 hours, or until cheese is melted and mixture is hot, stirring halfway through cooking.
3. Stir in ranch dip and peppers. Increase setting to HIGH. Cover and cook about 30 more minutes or until mixture is hot. Keep on LOW and serve with tortilla chips for dipping.

Did You Know?

Slow cookers are perfect when entertaining since we can get things cooking and almost forget about them. By the time the guests arrive, everything is ready. And because we can serve right from them, it means fewer dishes to wash.

Cocktail Smokies

Serves 10

1-½ cups barbecue sauce

¾ cup grape jelly

½ cup diced green bell pepper

1 (8-ounce) can pineapple tidbits, undrained

2 (16-ounce) packages miniature smoked sausage links

1. In a 2-½-quart or larger slow cooker, combine all ingredients; mix well.
2. Cook on LOW 4 to 5 hours or on HIGH 2 to 3 hours, or until heated through. Keep on LOW to serve hot.

This sauce is so amazing that it's good with almost anything. (Well, almost.) For a change of pace, feel free to try this with cocktail hotdogs or pre-cooked mini meatballs instead of the sausage.

Slow "Roasted" Chick Peas

Makes 2-½ cups

- 2 (15-ounce) cans chick peas, drained
- 2 tablespoons olive oil
- 2 teaspoons garlic powder
- 2 teaspoons salt

1. Rinse chick peas, place on paper towels, and pat dry.
2. In a medium bowl, combine olive oil, garlic powder, and salt; add chick peas and toss until evenly coated. Place in 2-½-quart or larger slow cooker.
3. Cover and cook on HIGH 4 hours, or until chick peas are dried and slightly browned, stirring occasionally. Remove to a baking sheet and let cool. Store any leftovers in an airtight container.

Good for You!

Chick peas, also known as garbanzo beans, are a great snack since they are packed with about 15 grams of protein per cup. So eat up, without any guilt!

Aunt Eileen's Sweet & Sour Meatballs

Serves 10

- 1 (14-ounce) can whole berry cranberry sauce
- 1 cup spaghetti sauce
- ⅓ cup packed brown sugar
- 1 (14.4-ounce) can sauerkraut
- 2 pounds frozen small meatballs (not thawed)

1. In a medium bowl, combine cranberry sauce, spaghetti sauce, brown sugar, and sauerkraut. Place frozen meatballs in a 5-quart or larger slow cooker and cover evenly with the sauce.
2. Cook on LOW 3 to 4 hours or on HIGH 2 hours, or until the meatballs are heated through. Keep on LOW to serve hot.

Did You Know?

The combo of the sweet cranberry sauce and brown sugar against the tartness of the sauerkraut makes these taste like some of the best stuffed cabbage we've ever had. Really!

Card Party Kielbasa

Serves 8

- ½ cup ketchup
- 2 tablespoons prepared horseradish
- 1 tablespoon Worcestershire sauce
- ¾ cup packed brown sugar
- 1 teaspoon dried mustard
- 2 pounds kielbasa sausage, thinly sliced

1. In a 4-quart or larger slow cooker, combine ketchup, horseradish, Worcestershire sauce, brown sugar, and mustard; mix well. Stir in kielbasa.

2. Cover and cook on LOW 1 to 1-½ hours, or until sauce is hot and begins to thicken. Keep on LOW to serve hot.

Did You Know?

These got their name since Howard's grandmother's longtime friend, Anna, used to serve these whenever the girls came over to play cards. Just make sure you wash your hands well after eating them or you might find the cards sticking to your fingers.

Sugar 'n' Spice Nut Mix

Serves 16

- 1 cup whole cashews
- 1 cup whole almonds
- 1 cup pecan halves
- 1 cup peanuts
- ½ cup sugar
- ¼ cup butter, melted
- 1 teaspoon ground cinnamon
- ½ teaspoon ground cloves
- ½ teaspoon salt
- ¼ teaspoon cayenne pepper

1. Place all nuts in a 2-½-quart or larger slow cooker.
2. In a small bowl, combine, sugar, butter, cinnamon, cloves, salt, and cayenne pepper. Sprinkle the nuts with the sugar mixture and toss to coat.
3. Cover and cook on LOW 1-½ hours, stirring after about 1 hour and again at end of cooking time.
4. Coat a baking sheet with cooking spray. Spread nuts in a single layer and let cool at least 1 hour. Store in an airtight container at room temperature up to 3 weeks.

These may seem a bit soft right after they've been cooked, but we discovered that once they cool, they get nice and crispy. Happy nibbling!

New Orleans Barbecue Shrimp

Serves 8

- 1 stick butter
- ¼ cup chicken broth
- ¼ cup Worcestershire sauce
- ¼ cup fresh lemon juice
- 4 cloves garlic, sliced
- 1 tablespoon seafood seasoning
- 1 teaspoon paprika
- ¼ teaspoon crushed red pepper
- ½ teaspoon salt
- ½ teaspoon black pepper
- 2 pounds large shrimp in shells, thawed if frozen

1. In a 5-quart or larger slow cooker, combine all ingredients except shrimp.
2. Cover and cook on HIGH 1-½ hours, or until bubbling. Stir in the shrimp, cover, and cook 30 minutes longer, or until shrimp are pink.
3. Remove to a serving dish and serve immediately with the broth on the side for dipping the peeled shrimp.

Serving Suggestion:
Make sure you put out empty bowls for the shells since this is one of those messy but fun peel-your-own kind of dishes. Extra napkins are also a good idea...trust us.

Fall-Off-the-Bone Chicken Wings

Serves 8

- 5 pounds chicken wings, thawed if frozen
- 1 (12-ounce) bottle chili sauce
- ½ cup orange marmalade
- ¼ cup molasses
- 2 tablespoons Worcestershire sauce
- 1 teaspoon hot pepper sauce
- 2 tablespoons lemon juice
- 2 tablespoons brown sugar
- 2 teaspoons garlic powder
- 2 teaspoons salt

1. Place chicken wings in a 6-quart or larger slow cooker.
2. In a medium bowl, combine remaining ingredients; mix well. Pour over chicken and stir until evenly coated.
3. Cover and cook on LOW 6 hours or on HIGH 3 hours, or until wings are fork-tender. Keep on LOW to serve hot.

Did You Know?

Although we are big fans of crispy fried chicken wings, these slow cooked wings are truly fall-off-the-bone delicious. When we served these to our official taste-testers, there wasn't one left. There also wasn't an ounce of meat left on any of the bones...they were that good.

Company Fancy Pesto Cheesecake

Serves 10

- 1 (8-ounce) package cream cheese, softened
- ½ cup ricotta cheese
- 1 egg
- 2 tablespoons prepared pesto sauce
- ¼ cup grated Parmesan cheese
- 1 tablespoon sliced almonds

1. Line a 2-quart slow cooker with foil.
2. In a large bowl, combine cream cheese and ricotta cheese; blend well with electric mixer. Add the egg, beating on high until well mixed.
3. In a small bowl, combine pesto and Parmesan cheese. Stir into cream cheese mixture, then spoon into slow cooker.
4. Cover and cook on LOW 2 to 2-½ hours, or until center is set. Let cool slightly, then remove to a platter by lifting out the foil. Gently remove the foil. Sprinkle with almonds and serve warm or let cool to room temperature.

If you don't have a 2-quart slow cooker, don't worry, you can use a 2-cup oven-safe baking dish and place it inside a larger slow cooker.

10-Minute Mexican Cheese Dip

Makes about 4 cups

½ pound hot Italian turkey sausage, casing removed

1 (10-ounce) can diced tomatoes and green chilies, undrained

1 cup chunky salsa

1 (16-ounce) package prepared cheese product, cut into cubes (like Velveeta)

Tortilla chips for dipping

1. In a 4-quart or larger pressure cooker, sauté sausage over medium heat 8 to 10 minutes, or until browned, crumbling it as it cooks. Add remaining ingredients and stir.

2. Securely lock lid and over high heat, bring to full pressure; reduce heat just enough to maintain pressure for 5 minutes. Perform a quick release. Remove lid, stir and serve with tortilla chips.

If you're not a big fan of spicy things, no problem! You can use mild Italian turkey sausage, as well as mild salsa. No worries, it'll still be quite tasty!

If using an electric pressure cooker prepare as directed above except:

- In step 1, sauté according to manufacturer's directions for your model.
- In step 2, set timer for 5 minutes.

For more details about how to use an electric pressure cooker, see pages xv-xvi.

Our Fastest Caponata

Makes about 6 cups

- 2 tablespoons olive oil
- 2 cloves garlic, minced
- 1 large eggplant, chopped (about 1-½ pounds)
- 1 onion, chopped (about 1 cup)
- ½ teaspoon salt
- ½ cup pitted green olives, coarsely chopped
- 3 stalks celery, chopped
- 1 (8-ounce) can tomato sauce
- ¼ cup white vinegar
- ⅓ cup packed brown sugar
- ¼ cup water

1. In a 4-quart or larger pressure cooker, heat oil; sauté garlic 2 to 3 minutes, or until golden. Add remaining ingredients and stir.
2. Securely lock lid and over high heat, bring to full pressure; reduce heat just enough to maintain pressure for 5 minutes. Perform a quick release.
3. Transfer to a serving bowl and cool to room temperature before serving.

Serving Suggestion:
Serve this like the restaurants do by putting out slices of toasted focaccia or French bread that's been toasted and rubbed with a little fresh garlic. Magnifico!

If using an electric pressure cooker prepare as directed above except:

- In step 1, sauté according to manufacturer's directions for your model.
- In step 2, set timer for 5 minutes.

For more details about how to use an electric pressure cooker, see pages xv-xvi.

Buffalo Chicken Meatballs

PRESSURE COOKER

Serves 8

- 1-½ pounds ground chicken
- 1 cup Panko bread crumbs
- 1 egg
- 1 teaspoon onion powder
- 1 teaspoon celery salt
- ½ teaspoon black pepper
- ½ cup thinly sliced celery
- ⅓ cup sliced scallions
- 2 tablespoons oil
- 1 cup buffalo wing sauce
- ½ cup water
- ½ cup blue cheese dressing

1. In a large bowl, gently combine chicken, bread crumbs, egg, onion powder, celery salt, pepper, celery, and scallions. Mix well and form into 24 cocktail-sized meatballs.
2. In a 5-quart or larger pressure cooker, heat oil on HIGH, until hot. Place meatballs into oil and cook, in batches, until browned on all sides. Once all meatballs are browned, return them to the pressure cooker. Pour buffalo sauce and water over meatballs.
3. Securely lock lid and over high heat, bring to full pressure; reduce heat just enough to maintain pressure for 6 minutes. Perform a natural release.
4. Remove lid and serve with blue cheese dressing for dipping.

If using an electric pressure cooker prepare as directed above except:

- In step 2, cook according to manufacturer's directions for your model.
- In step 3, set timer for 6 minutes.

For more details about how to use an electric pressure cooker, see pages xv-xvi.

Steamed Artichokes with Lemon Yogurt Sauce

Serves 4

- 2 large artichokes
- 1 lemon, cut in half
- 1 cup water
- ¼ cup Greek yogurt
- ½ clove garlic, finely chopped
- 2 teaspoons lemon juice
- 1-½ teaspoons chopped fresh basil
- 1 teaspoon Worcestershire sauce
- 1 teaspoon Dijon mustard
- ⅛ teaspoon salt
- ⅛ teaspoon black pepper

1. Trim artichokes by cutting off top edges of leaves with scissors. Trim stem so it sits flat. Rub lemon on any cut edges to prevent them from browning.

2. Add water to 4-quart or larger pressure cooker. Place artichokes in steamer basket, and place into pressure cooker. Squeeze lemon over top each artichoke.

3. Securely lock lid and over high heat, bring to full pressure; reduce heat just enough to maintain pressure for 10 minutes. Perform a natural release. (Check an outer leaf for doneness. If not tender, put lid on loosely and continue cooking on medium-low for a few more minutes.)

4. Meanwhile, in a small bowl, whisk together remaining ingredients. Serve with artichokes for dipping.

If using an electric pressure cooker prepare as directed above except:

- In step 3, set timer for 10 minutes. If leaves are still tough, put lid on loosely and set timer for a few more minutes.

For more details about how to use an electric pressure cooker, see pages xv-xvi.

Caramelized Garlic

PRESSURE COOKER

Makes 3 bulbs

3 large garlic bulbs

1 cup water

1 tablespoon olive oil

1. Slice ¼-inch off tops of garlic bulbs. Add water to a 4-quart or larger pressure cooker. Place garlic in steamer basket, and place into pressure cooker.
2. Securely lock lid and over high heat, bring to full pressure; reduce heat just enough to maintain pressure for 8 minutes. Perform a natural release.
3. Meanwhile, preheat oven to broil. Using tongs, remove soft garlic bulbs and place on baking sheet. Drizzle with oil and broil 6 to 8 minutes, or until golden and caramelized.

Serving Suggestion:

Caramelized garlic is great just slathered on French bread, but you can also mix it into mashed potatoes or anywhere you want a sweet, nutty, mild garlic flavor.

If using an electric pressure cooker prepare as directed above except:

- In step 2, set timer for 8 minutes.

For more details about how to use an electric pressure cooker, see pages xv-xvi.

Mr. Food
TEST KITCHEN

Hot Stuff in a Bowl

All-in-One Lasagna Soup

Serves 6

- 1-¼ pounds Italian sausage, casings removed
- ½ cup chopped onion
- 1 (28-ounce) can diced tomatoes
- 4 cups chicken broth
- 2 cups spaghetti sauce
- 6 cloves garlic, minced
- 2 teaspoons Italian seasoning
- 8 dried lasagna noodles, broken into 1-inch pieces
- 1 cup ricotta cheese
- ¼ cup Parmesan cheese

1. In a large skillet over high heat, sauté sausage and onion until browned, stirring occasionally to crumble sausage.
2. In a 6-quart or larger slow cooker, combine sausage mixture, tomatoes, broth, spaghetti sauce, garlic, and Italian seasoning. Stir to combine.
3. Cook on LOW 7 hours or on HIGH 3 hours. Stir in the pasta. Cover and cook 30 to 45 more minutes, or until pasta is tender.
4. Ladle into bowls and evenly top each with a dollop of ricotta cheese and a shake or two or Parmesan cheese.

We tested this with several types of pasta and although they all work, we suggest using the lasagna noodles as directed, or bowties, which give this the same lasagna feel without having to break them up.

White Bean & Sausage Soup

SLOW COOKER

Serves 6

- 1 pound hot pork sausage, casings removed
- 4 cups chopped kale
- 1 onion, chopped
- 2 (16-ounce) cans cannellini beans
- 4 cups beef broth
- 1 (28-ounce) can crushed tomatoes, undrained
- 1 teaspoon ground cumin
- 1 teaspoon salt
- ½ teaspoon black pepper

1. In a large skillet over medium-high heat, cook sausage 6 to 8 minutes, or until no longer pink, stirring to crumble. Drain excess liquid and transfer to a 5-quart or larger slow cooker. Add remaining ingredients and stir well.

2. Cover and cook on LOW 8 to 9 hours or on HIGH 6 hours, or until kale is tender.

Good for You!
Kale has been elevated from just a salad bar garnish to a popular addition to our diets, and we can feel good knowing that it's packed with all sorts of vitamins, including whopping amounts of vitamins A, C, and K.

South-of-the-Border Taco Soup

Serves 8

- 1 tablespoon vegetable oil
- 1 pound ground beef
- 1 onion, chopped
- 1 (1.25-ounce) package taco seasoning
- 2 tablespoons water
- 1 (16-ounce) can chili beans, undrained
- 1 (15-ounce) can black beans, drained and rinsed
- 2 cups frozen corn
- 1 (8-ounce) can tomato sauce
- 2 cups beef broth
- 1 (10-ounce) can diced tomatoes with chilies, undrained

1. In a large skillet over medium-high heat, heat oil; cook ground beef and onion until no pink remains, stirring to crumble beef as it cooks. Drain excess liquid. Stir in taco seasoning and water.

2. Place the beans, corn, tomato sauce, broth, and diced tomatoes into a 5-quart or larger slow cooker. Spoon beef mixture over top.

3. Cover and cook on LOW 7 hours or on HIGH 3 hours, or until bubbling.

Serving Suggestion:

Make serving this extra fun by putting out bowls of all your favorite taco toppings like shredded cheese, sour cream, and of course, some crushed tortilla chips.

Super Simple Veggie Soup

Serves 6

- 2 cloves garlic, minced
- 1 onion, chopped
- 1 green bell pepper, diced
- 2 stalks celery, diced
- 2 (15-ounce) cans Italian-style diced tomatoes, undrained
- 1 (16-ounce) package mixed frozen vegetables
- 5 cups beef broth
- 2 tablespoons soy sauce
- 3 tablespoons Worcestershire sauce
- 1 teaspoon paprika
- 1 teaspoon salt
- ½ teaspoon black pepper
- 1 cup dry ditalini pasta

1. In a 5-quart or larger slow cooker, add all ingredients except pasta and Parmesan cheese; stir to combine.
2. Cover and cook on LOW 6 to 8 hours or on HIGH 4 hours. During the last 30 to 45 minutes of cooking, stir in pasta and cook until pasta is tender.

Want to make this vegetarian? Simply substitute vegetable broth for the beef broth. How simple is that? Plus, to give this an extra wow, finish each bowl off with a bit of grated Parmesan cheese.

Slow Cookin' Chicken 'n' Corn Soup

Serves 6

- 2 cups chicken broth
- 2 (10-3/4-ounce) cans cream of chicken soup, undiluted
- 1 (16-ounce) package frozen corn
- 3 boneless skinless chicken breasts, cut into 1/2-inch chunks
- 1 (10-ounce) can diced tomatoes with green chilies
- 1 (8-1/2-ounce) can cream-style corn
- 8 ounces prepared cheese product, cubed (like Velveeta)
- 1 teaspoon garlic powder
- 1/4 teaspoon black pepper
- 1 tablespoon chopped fresh cilantro

1. In a 5-quart or larger slow cooker, stir together broth and cream of chicken soup until blended. Add remaining ingredients except cilantro.

2. Cover and cook on LOW 5 hours or on HIGH 2-1/2 hours, or until chicken is no longer pink. Ladle into bowls, sprinkle with cilantro, and serve.

Serving Suggestion:
Like things a bit spicy? Top this soup with some chopped pickled jalapeños or a few dashes of hot sauce.

Old-Fashioned Potato Soup

Serves 6

- 4 tablespoons (½ stick) butter
- 1-½ cups diced onion
- 2-½ pounds potatoes, diced
- 2 cups chicken broth
- 1 teaspoon salt
- ½ teaspoon black pepper
- 2 cups milk
- 1 cup frozen peas
- ½ cup potato flakes

1. In a skillet over medium heat, melt butter; sauté onion until brown
2. In a 5-quart or larger slow cooker, combine onions, potatoes, broth, salt, and pepper.
3. Cover and cook on LOW 5 to 6 hours or on HIGH 3 hours, or until potatoes are fork- tender.
4. Stir in milk, peas, and potato flakes, and continue cooking 30 minutes, uncovered, or until mixture is thickened and heated through.

Did You Know?

Using potato flakes not only helps thicken this soup, but it can also be used to thicken sauces and gravies in a pinch.

Velvety Tomato & Rice Soup

Serves 6

- 2 (28-ounce) cans crushed tomatoes
- 1 tablespoon sugar
- ½ teaspoon garlic powder
- 1 teaspoon salt
- 1 teaspoon black pepper
- 2 cups (1 pint) heavy cream
- 1-½ cups warm cooked white rice

1. In a 5-quart or larger slow cooker, combine tomatoes, sugar, garlic powder, salt, and pepper.
2. Cook on LOW 6 hours or on HIGH 3 hours. During the last 15 to 20 minutes of cooking, slowly stir in the heavy cream and rice. Cook, uncovered, until heated through.

Sure you can use leftover rice, or you can buy precooked packaged rice in your supermarket. Either way, just make sure you warm it up before adding it to the soup.

Mama Marie's Wedding Soup

Serves 8

- 6 (10.5-ounce) cans condensed chicken broth
- 4 cups water
- 1 pound frozen meatballs
- 4 cups fresh chopped escarole or spinach
- ¾ cup grated Parmesan cheese, plus extra for garnish
- 2 eggs, beaten

1. In a 6-quart or larger slow cooker, combine broth, water, and meatballs. Cover and cook on LOW 6 to 7 hours or on HIGH 3 to 4 hours.
2. Remove cover and gradually stir in beaten egg, forming thin strands. Stir in escarole and ¾ cup Parmesan cheese. Serve immediately topped with additional Parmesan cheese.

Food for Thought:

Most people think this soup got its name by being served at Italian weddings. That is not the case. The translation of the name actually refers to the marriage of the meatballs and greens, not the bride and groom. See, ya learn something new every day.

Really Tender Moroccan Stew

Serves 5

- 1 tablespoon vegetable oil
- 2 pounds boneless, skinless chicken thighs, cut into 1-inch chunks
- 2 cups chicken broth
- ½ cup dried apricots, slivered
- ½ cup green olives, drained and cut in half
- 2 tablespoons capers, drained
- 1 teaspoon chopped garlic
- 1 tablespoon chopped parsley
- ¼ cup brown sugar
- 2 tablespoons dried oregano
- 1-½ teaspoons salt
- ½ teaspoon black pepper
- ⅓ cup red wine vinegar
- 1 tablespoon cornstarch
- 2 tablespoons water

1. In a large skillet over medium-high heat, heat oil. Add chicken and cook 5 minutes, or until browned. Place in a 4-quart or larger slow cooker.

2. Cover and cook on LOW 4 to 5 hours or on HIGH 2-½ hours. Add broth, apricots, olives, capers, garlic, parsley, brown sugar, oregano, salt, pepper, and vinegar; mix well. Cover and cook on HIGH 1 additional hour.

3. In a small bowl, whisk together cornstarch and water until smooth; whisk into slow cooker. Cover and cook on HIGH 5 more minutes, or until sauce is thickened.

Serving Suggestion:
We think this is best over hot cooked rice or couscous so it can soak up all the flavor-packed sauce.

Loaded Jambalaya Stew

Serves 6

- 1-½ pounds boneless, skinless chicken thighs, cut into 1-inch pieces
- 1 tablespoon Creole seasoning
- 2 tablespoons vegetable oil
- ½ cup chopped onion
- ½ cup chopped celery
- ½ cup chopped green bell pepper
- 1 (14-½-ounce) can diced tomatoes
- 1-¾ cups chicken broth
- 2 cups cooked rice
- 1 pound smoked sausage, cut on the diagonal into 1-inch pieces
- 1 pound medium fresh shrimp, peeled and deveined
- ½ cup chopped scallions
- 1 tablespoon hot sauce

1. Sprinkle chicken evenly with Creole seasoning. In a large skillet over high heat, heat oil. Add chicken and cook 4 to 5 minutes, or until browned, stirring occasionally.

2. Spoon chicken into a 5-quart or larger slow cooker. Add onion, celery, bell pepper, tomatoes, and broth.

3. Cover and cook on LOW 6 hours or on HIGH 3 hours. Stir in rice, smoked sausage, shrimp, scallions, and hot sauce. Cover and cook on HIGH 10 to 15 minutes, or until shrimp turn pink.

Make sure you cook the shrimp until just pink. Overcooking can cause them to get rubbery and they will shrink down to nothing.

Thursday Night Beef Stew

Serves 6

- ¼ cup all-purpose flour
- 1 teaspoon salt, divided
- 1 teaspoon black pepper, divided
- 2 pounds beef stew meat, cut into 1-inch cubes
- 1-½ cups beef broth
- 3 cloves garlic, minced
- ½ teaspoon dried thyme
- 2 tablespoons Worcestershire sauce
- 1 onion, sliced into half moons
- 4 potatoes, cut into 1-inch chunks
- 5 carrots, cut into 1-inch chunks

1. In a large bowl, combine flour, ½ teaspoon salt, and ½ teaspoon pepper; add beef and toss to coat evenly.
2. Place beef into a 6-quart or larger slow cooker. Add remaining ingredients, including remaining salt and pepper; stir gently.
3. Cover and cook on LOW 9 to 10 hours or on HIGH 4 to 5 hours, or until the meat is tender.

Howard Says:

"Growing up, my mom seemed to make this almost every Thursday night. It was so common, that after a few weeks my brother and I started calling this Thursday night beef stew. Now, all these years later, the name has stuck, and yes, it's still as good as I remember."

Hearty White Bean Chili

Serves 8

- 1 tablespoon vegetable oil
- 1 pound ground turkey breast
- 1 onion, chopped
- 2 cloves garlic, minced
- 3 (15.5-ounce) cans Great Northern Beans, undrained
- 1 (14-½-ounce) can diced tomatoes, undrained
- 1 (8-ounce) can tomato sauce
- 1 (4-ounce) can chopped green chilies, undrained
- 2 teaspoons ground cumin
- 1-½ teaspoons chili powder

1. In a large skillet over medium heat, heat oil; sauté turkey, onion, and garlic 6 to 8 minutes, or until turkey is no longer pink. Place turkey mixture in a 5-quart or larger slow cooker, and add remaining ingredients; stir.

2. Cover and cook on LOW 8 hours or on HIGH 4 hours, or until chili is slightly thickened.

Good for You!

Using heart-healthier ground turkey breast rather than ground beef in this recipe will save you more than 100 calories and 6 grams of saturated fat per serving, without losing flavor!

Aunt Helen's Cabbage Soup

PRESSURE COOKER

Serves 6

- 4 cups beef broth
- 1 tablespoon lemon juice
- 1-½ pounds beef top round or beef chuck roast, cut into 1-inch chunks
- ½ head green cabbage (about 1 pound), coarsely chopped
- ½ teaspoon salt
- 1 (28-ounce) can crushed tomatoes
- 1 (6-ounce) can tomato paste
- ½ cup packed brown sugar

1. In a 6-quart or larger pressure cooker, add all ingredients in order listed, do not stir.
2. Securely lock lid and over high heat, bring to full pressure; reduce heat just enough to maintain pressure for 10 minutes. Perform a natural release.
3. Remove cover, stir and serve.

Did You Know?

This sauce gets its sweet and sour tang from the combo of the brown sugar and lemon juice. The two opposites really complement each other when cooked together. Oh, and don't forget the pumpernickel bread for dunkin' like my Aunt Helen used to use.

If using an electric pressure cooker prepare as directed above except:

- In step 2, set timer for 10 minutes.

For more details about how to use an electric pressure cooker, *see pages xv-xvi.*

Lightning Quick Tortilla Soup

Serves 6

- 1 tablespoon vegetable oil
- 1 pound boneless, skinless chicken breasts, cut into ½-inch cubes
- 1 red bell pepper, coarsely chopped
- 3 cloves garlic, minced
- 7 cups chicken broth
- 2 cups frozen corn
- ¾ cup salsa
- 2 (6-inch) flour tortillas, cut into ¼-inch strips
- ¼ cup chopped fresh cilantro

1 In a 6-quart or larger pressure cooker over medium heat, heat oil. Add chicken, bell pepper, and garlic and sauté 3 to 5 minutes, or until chicken is no longer pink, stirring frequently. Stir in chicken broth, corn, and salsa.

2 Securely lock lid and over high heat, bring to full pressure; reduce heat just enough to maintain pressure for 8 minutes. Perform a natural release.

3 Remove lid from pressure cooker and stir in tortilla strips and cilantro; let sit 2 to 3 minutes to soften, then serve.

Did You Know?

Once the tortillas hit the hot soup, they puff up and become just like noodles. How fun is that?

If using an electric pressure cooker prepare as directed above except:

- In step 1, sauté according to manufacturer's directions for your model.
- In step 2, set timer for 8 minutes.

For more details about how to use an electric pressure cooker, see pages xv-xvi.

5-Minute Noodle Soup

Serves 10

- 6 (10.5-ounce) cans condensed chicken broth
- 2 tablespoons soy sauce, divided
- 2 cups sliced mushrooms
- 1 (15-ounce) can baby corn, drained and cut in thirds
- 1-½ cups shredded carrot
- 2 pound boneless, skinless chicken breasts, cut into ½-inch chunks
- 4 ounces uncooked spaghetti, broken in half
- 1 cup fresh snow peas, trimmed
- 2 scallions, sliced

1. In a 6-quart or larger pressure cooker, combine chicken broth, 1 tablespoon soy sauce, mushrooms, baby corn, carrot, and chicken.
2. Securely lock lid and over high heat, bring to full pressure; reduce heat just enough to maintain pressure for 5 minutes. Perform a natural release.
3. Remove lid from pressure cooker and stir in spaghetti, snow peas, and remaining soy sauce. Simmer over medium heat, uncovered, 7 to 9 minutes, or until spaghetti is tender, stirring occasionally. Top each serving with scallions.

Although we are big fans of cooking pasta in a pressure cooker, we think this recipe works best if you cook it after, but in the same pot. This way it doesn't absorb too much of the broth.

If using an electric pressure cooker prepare as directed above except:

- In step 2, set timer for 5 minutes.
- In step 3, simmer according to manufacturer's directions for your model.

For more details about how to use an electric pressure cooker, see pages xv-xvi.

Lumberjack Soup

Serves 8

- 2 cups peeled and chopped butternut squash
- 1 onion, chopped
- 4 cloves garlic, minced
- 1 cup wild rice
- 4 cups chicken broth
- 2 cups water
- 1 tablespoon chopped fresh rosemary
- ½ teaspoon salt
- ¼ teaspoon black pepper
- 2 cups chopped kale
- 1 (14-ounce) package kielbasa sausage, cut into half-moon slices

1 In a 6-quart or larger pressure cooker, combine squash, onion, garlic, wild rice, broth, water, rosemary, salt, and pepper.

2 Securely lock lid and over high heat, bring to full pressure; reduce heat just enough to maintain pressure for 15 minutes. Perform a natural release.

3 Remove lid and stir in kale and kielbasa; simmer over medium heat 5 to 7 minutes, or until kale is tender and kielbasa is heated through. Serve immediately.

We found the best way to peel the butternut squash is with a good old-fashioned vegetable peeler. After it's peeled, cut it in half lengthwise, scoop out the seeds, and you're ready to cut it up.

If using an electric pressure cooker prepare as directed above except:

- In step 2, set timer for 15 minutes. In step 3, simmer according to manufacturer's directions for your model.

For more details about how to use an electric pressure cooker, see pages xv-xvi.

Split Second Pea Soup

Serves 6

- 1 (16-ounce) package split peas
- ½ pound deli ham, cut into ½-inch chunks
- 3 carrots, cut into ¼-inch slices
- 2 stalks celery, cut into ¼-inch slices
- 1 onion, diced
- 1 bay leaf
- 1-½ teaspoons salt
- ½ teaspoon black pepper
- 3 cups chicken broth
- 3 cups water

1 Place all ingredients in a 5-quart or larger pressure cooker; mix well.

2 Securely lock lid and over high heat, bring to full pressure; reduce heat just enough to maintain pressure for 10 minutes. Perform a natural release.

3 Remove and discard bay leaf, stir, and serve immediately.

Howard Says:

"My grandmother used to make pea soup in a pressure cooker all the time. It was her go to soup except she used to put in chunks of beef flanken instead of the ham. Let me tell you that when I tasted this...it sure brought back some pretty amazing memories. I sure miss her and her cooking."

If using an electric pressure cooker prepare as directed above except:

- In step 2, set timer for 10 minutes.

For more details about how to use an electric pressure cooker, see pages xv-xvi.

Steak Dinner Soup

Serves 6

- 2 tablespoons vegetable oil
- 1-½ pounds boneless beef top sirloin steak (½-inch thick), trimmed and cut into thin strips (see Tip)
- ½ pound fresh mushrooms, sliced
- 1 large onion, chopped
- 7 cups beef broth
- 1 cup water
- ½ cup dry red wine
- 3 large potatoes, unpeeled and cut into ½-inch cubes
- 2 teaspoons steak seasoning
- ½ cup French-fried onions

1 In a 6-quart or larger pressure cooker over medium-high heat, heat oil. Add steak strips, mushrooms, and onion and sauté 6 to 8 minutes, or until steak is browned and onion is tender. Add remaining ingredients except French fried onions.

2 Securely lock lid in place and over high heat, bring to full pressure; reduce heat just enough to maintain pressure for 10 minutes. Perform a natural release.

3 Ladle soup into bowls and sprinkle with French fried onions. Serve immediately.

Sure you can buy a sirloin steak and cut it up yourself or if you prefer, ask the butcher at the market to do it for you. We're sure they'll be happy to and it'll save you some time.

If using an electric pressure cooker prepare as directed above except:

- In step 1, sauté according to manufacturer's directions for your model.
- In step 2, set timer for 10 minutes.

For more details about how to use an electric pressure cooker, see pages xv-xvi.

Naked Onion Soup

Serves 6

- 1 stick butter
- 6 onions, cut in half and thinly sliced
- 1 tablespoon brown sugar
- 1-½ teaspoons salt
- ½ teaspoon black pepper
- 3 (10.5-ounce) cans condensed beef broth
- 1 cup apple cider
- ½ cup red wine

1. In a large skillet over medium-high heat, melt butter; add onions, brown sugar, salt, and pepper. Sauté 12 to 15 minutes, or until golden brown, stirring occasionally.
2. Place onions in a 4-1/2 quart or larger pressure cooker, and stir in remaining ingredients.
3. Securely lock lid and over high heat, bring to full pressure; reduce heat just enough to maintain pressure for 4 minutes. Perform a natural release. Serve immediately.

Did You Know?

We call this naked since we don't cover it up with bread and melted cheese like we normally would. You could say it's so good, we can enjoy this au naturel! And by the way, we sauté the onions in a skillet because there's a lot of them. You could sauté them in your pressure cooker. It'll just take a bit longer.

If using an electric pressure cooker prepare as directed above except:

- In step 3, set timer for 4 minutes.

For more details about how to use an electric pressure cooker, see pages xv-xvi.

Butternut Squash Soup

Serves 4

- 5 cups peeled butternut squash chunks
- 1 apple, peeled and diced
- 1 cup sliced celery
- ½ cup chopped onion
- 1 cup coconut milk
- 1 cup chicken broth
- ⅛ teaspoon ground nutmeg
- ½ teaspoon salt
- ¼ teaspoon black pepper

1. Place all ingredients in a 6-quart or larger pressure cooker.
2. Securely lock lid and over high heat, bring to full pressure; reduce heat just enough to maintain pressure for 15 minutes. Perform a natural release. Stir until smooth and serve immediately.

Did You Know?
By making this in a pressure cooker rather than a tradition soup pot, it's done in 75% less time and the flavor is so much richer. Ah, that is why we love our pressure cookers!

If using an electric pressure cooker prepare as directed above except:

- In step 2, set timer for 15 minutes.

For more details about how to use an electric pressure cooker, *see pages xv-xvi.*

Really Good Chicken Broth

Makes 2 quarts

- 3 pounds chicken wings
- 3 carrots, cut into 1-inch pieces
- 2 celery stalks, cut into 1-inch pieces
- 1 onion, cut into 1-inch pieces
- 1 tablespoon kosher salt
- ½ teaspoon whole black peppercorns

1. Place all ingredients in a 6-quart or larger pressure cooker. Pour in enough water just to cover ingredients. (Do not fill above pressure cooker's "maximum fill" line.)
2. Securely lock lid and over high heat, bring to full pressure; reduce heat just enough to maintain pressure for 40 minutes. Perform a natural release.
3. Strain broth over a pot or heat-proof bowl. Refrigerate broth overnight, or until the fat solidifies on the top. Remove fat and discard. Store broth in an airtight container in the refrigerator up to 3 days, or freeze up to 6 months.

Food For Thought:

In today's fast-paced world, making stock or broth from scratch is almost unheard of. Sure it's nice to have the convenience of premade broth, but nothing is as good as the real deal. And thanks to our pressure cooker we can have the richest broth in less than an hour. Sure beats cooking it all day long!

If using an electric pressure cooker prepare as directed above except:

- In step 2, set timer for 40 minutes.

For more details about how to use an electric pressure cooker, see pages xv-xvi.

Bubblin' Brunswick Stew

Serves 4

- 1-½ cups chicken broth
- 1 (14-½ ounce) can diced tomatoes, undrained
- 2 pounds boneless skinless chicken thighs
- 5 carrots, cut into ½-inch chunks
- 1 onion, chopped
- 2 bay leaves
- ½ teaspoon dried thyme
- 1-½ teaspoons salt
- ¼ teaspoon cayenne pepper
- 1 (15.5-ounce) can Great Northern beans, drained
- 1 (14.75-ounce) can cream-style corn
- 2 cups frozen cut okra, thawed

1. In a 6-quart or larger pressure cooker, combine broth, tomatoes, chicken, carrots, onion, bay leaves, thyme, salt, and cayenne pepper; mix well.

2. Securely lock lid and over high heat, bring to full pressure; reduce heat just enough to maintain pressure for 8 minutes. Perform a natural release.

3. Remove lid and remove the chicken thighs to a cutting board. Shred with 2 forks and place back in pressure cooker. Stir in remaining ingredients and simmer over medium-low heat, uncovered, about 10 minutes, or until heated through.

Did You Know?

There are hundreds of different versions of Brunswick Stew out there; the "authentic" ones call for squirrel, possum, or rabbit meat. We'll stick with the chicken version, thank you.

If using an electric pressure cooker prepare as directed above except:

- In step 2, set timer for 8 minutes.
- In step 3, simmer according to manufacturer's directions for your model.

For more details about how to use an electric pressure cooker, see pages xv-xvi.

Quick-as-a-Wink Beef Stew

Serves 4

- 1/4 cup all-purpose flour
- 2 teaspoons salt, divided
- 1 teaspoon black pepper, divided
- 2-1/2 pounds boneless beef chuck roast, cut into 1-inch cubes
- 2 tablespoons vegetable oil
- 5 potatoes (about 2 pounds), peeled and cut into quarters
- 5 carrots, cut into 1-inch chunks
- 1 onion, cut into wedges
- 1-1/2 cups beef broth
- 1 (14-ounce) can diced tomatoes
- 1/2 teaspoon browning and seasoning sauce

1. In a shallow dish, combine flour, 1 teaspoon salt, and 1/2 teaspoon pepper; add beef and toss until evenly coated.
2. In a 6-quart or larger pressure cooker over high heat, heat oil; add beef and any remaining flour mixture and sauté, uncovered, 8 to 10 minutes, or until meat is browned. Add remaining ingredients except browning and seasoning sauce.
3. Securely lock lid and over high heat bring to full pressure; reduce heat just enough to maintain pressure for 8 minutes. Perform a natural release.
4. Remove lid and stir in browning and seasoning sauce. Simmer over medium heat 5 minutes, or until sauce is slightly thickened.

If using an electric pressure cooker prepare as directed above except:

- In step 2, sauté according to manufacturer's directions for your model.
- In step 3, set timer for 8 minutes.
- In step 4, simmer according to manufacturer's directions for your model.

For more details about how to use an electric pressure cooker, see pages xv-xvi.

Italian Sausage Stew

Serves 6

- 1 pound Italian sausage, cut into 1-inch chunks
- 1 (15-ounce) can garbanzo beans, drained
- 1 (14.5-ounce) can diced tomatoes, undrained
- 3 cups chicken broth
- 1 cup lentils
- 1 onion, diced
- ¼ cup chopped fresh parsley
- 3 cloves garlic, minced
- 2 cups packed fresh spinach

1. In a 6-quart or larger pressure cooker, combine all ingredients except spinach; mix well.
2. Securely lock lid and over high heat, bring to full pressure; reduce heat just enough to maintain pressure for 9 minutes. Perform a quick release.
3. Remove lid, stir in spinach, and serve.

This recipe makes a lot. Why not enjoy any leftovers for lunch throughout the week?

If using an electric pressure cooker prepare as directed above except:

- In step 2, set timer for 9 minutes.

For more details about how to use an electric pressure cooker, *see pages xv-xvi.*

Chunky Beef 'n' Bean Chili

Serves 4

- ¼ cup vegetable oil
- 3 pounds boneless beef chuck steak or roast, cut into 1-inch cubes
- 4 large onions, coarsely chopped
- 4 garlic cloves, minced
- 1 (28-ounce) can crushed tomatoes
- 2 bay leaves
- 3 tablespoons chili powder
- 1-½ teaspoons ground cumin
- 1 teaspoon salt
- ⅛ teaspoon cayenne pepper
- 3 (15-ounce) cans red kidney beans, drained

1. In a 6-quart or larger pressure cooker over high heat, heat oil. Add beef and sauté, uncovered, 8 to 10 minutes, or until browned, stirring occasionally. Add remaining ingredients except kidney beans; mix well.

2. Securely lock lid and over high heat, bring to full pressure; reduce heat just enough to maintain pressure for 16 minutes. Perform a natural release.

3. Remove lid and stir in kidney beans. Simmer over medium-low heat, uncovered, 4 to 5 minutes, or until beans are heated through. Discard bay leaves before serving.

Serving Suggestion:
To finish off this real down-home chili, top each bowl with a dollop of sour cream, chopped onions, or shredded cheese – or better yet, all three!

If using an electric pressure cooker prepare as directed above except:

- In step 1, sauté according to manufacturer's directions for your model.
- In step 2, set timer for 16 minutes.
- In step 3, simmer according to manufacturer's directions for your model.

For more details about how to use an electric pressure cooker, see pages xv-xvi.

From the Hen House

Cilantro Lime Chicken Wraps

SLOW COOKER

Serves 6

- 1 (16-ounce) jar salsa
- 1 (15-ounce) can black beans, rinsed and drained
- 1-½ cups frozen corn
- 1 (1.25-ounce) packet dry taco seasoning mix
- 2 tablespoons lime juice
- 1 teaspoon lime zest
- ¼ cup chopped fresh cilantro
- 2 pounds boneless, skinless chicken breasts
- 6 (8-inch) flour tortillas, warmed
- Lime wedges for garnish (optional)

1. In a 5-quart or larger slow cooker, mix salsa, beans, corn, taco seasoning, lime juice, lime zest, and cilantro. Add chicken and stir to coat.

2. Cover and cook on LOW 6 to 8 hours or on HIGH about 4 hours, or until chicken is fall-apart tender. Remove chicken to a cutting board and shred with 2 forks. Place shredded chicken back in slow cooker and stir.

3. Serve in warmed tortillas and garnish with wedges of lime, if desired.

Cowboy BBQ Chicken Sandwiches

Serves 6

- 2-½ to 3 pounds boneless, skinless chicken thighs
- ½ cup diced onion
- 1 (12-ounce) bottle barbecue sauce
- ½ cup Italian dressing
- ¼ cup brown sugar
- 2 tablespoons Worcestershire sauce
- 6 kaiser rolls

1. In a 5-quart or larger slow cooker, place chicken. In a bowl, mix the remaining ingredients except rolls; evenly pour over chicken.

2. Cover and cook on LOW 6 to 8 hours or on HIGH 3 to 4 hours, or until chicken is fall-apart tender.

3. Remove chicken to a cutting board and shred using 2 forks. Return to slow cooker and stir to coat. Cut the rolls in half and toast. Spoon shredded chicken onto rolls and enjoy.

If you have some leftover pulled chicken, you can use it to top prebaked pizza shells along with some shredded Cheddar for BBQ chicken pizzas.

Italian Chicken 'n' Veggie Toss

Serves 4

- 3 cups frozen asparagus, peppers, peas and carrots blend
- 1-½ pounds boneless, skinless chicken breasts, cut into 1-inch pieces
- ¼ teaspoon salt
- ¼ teaspoon black pepper
- 2 cups spaghetti sauce
- 2 tablespoons tomato paste
- 2 garlic cloves, minced
- 1 teaspoon Italian seasoning
- ¼ cup cooking sherry or chicken broth
- 2 tablespoons Parmesan cheese

1. Place frozen vegetables in a 5-quart or larger slow cooker. Sprinkle chicken with salt and pepper, and place over vegetables.

2. In a large bowl, mix spaghetti sauce, tomato paste, garlic, Italian seasoning, and sherry. Pour over chicken.

3. Cover and cook on LOW 4 to 5 hours, or until chicken is cooked through and fork-tender. Sprinkle with Parmesan cheese and serve.

Rather than storing your leftover tomato paste in the fridge, place it in an ice cube tray and freeze it. Then the next time, just add it right into whatever you're making without even thawing it. How easy is that?

Chicken Rustica

Serves 4

- 4 tablespoons olive oil, divided
- 1 (3-pound) chicken, cut into 8 pieces
- 1-½ cups sliced baby portobella mushrooms
- 1 onion, diced
- 2 cloves garlic, minced
- 1 cup chicken broth
- 1 (6-ounce) can tomato paste
- ⅓ cup dry red wine
- 2 teaspoons sugar
- 1 teaspoon oregano
- ½ teaspoon salt
- ¼ teaspoon black pepper
- 2 tablespoons slivered fresh basil

1. In a skillet over medium heat, heat 2 tablespoons oil until hot. Brown half the chicken pieces on each side 3 to 5 minutes, turning once. Remove, add remaining oil, and brown remaining chicken; set aside.

2. Place mushrooms, onion, and garlic in a 6-quart or larger slow cooker and top with chicken pieces. In a bowl, combine broth, tomato paste, wine, sugar, oregano, salt, and pepper. Pour over chicken.

3. Cover and cook on LOW 7 to 8 hours or on HIGH 3 to 4 hours, or until chicken is cooked through and no pink remains. Top with basil and serve.

We discovered that browning the chicken adds a rich flavor to the dish even though a lot of the brown color fades away during the moist cooking process.

Sweet & Sour Chicken

Serves 4

- ¼ cup plus 3 tablespoons chicken broth, divided
- 3 tablespoons hoisin sauce
- 2 tablespoons low-sodium soy sauce
- 1 tablespoon tomato paste
- 1 tablespoon cider vinegar
- 1 tablespoon brown sugar
- 1 garlic clove, minced
- 1-½ to 2 pounds boneless, skinless chicken thighs, cut into 1-inch pieces
- 2 green bell peppers, cut into 1-inch chunks
- 2 tablespoons cornstarch
- 1 (8-ounce) can pineapple chunks, drained
- ¼ cup maraschino cherries, halved
- 4 cups cooked rice

1. In a 4-quart or larger slow cooker, combine ¼ cup broth, the hoisin sauce, soy sauce, tomato paste, vinegar, brown sugar, and garlic; mix well. Add chicken and green pepper, and stir to coat completely.
2. Cover and cook on LOW 2-½ to 3-½ hours.
3. In a small bowl, combine cornstarch and remaining chicken broth. Slowly stir into chicken along with pineapple and cherries. With the lid off, turn heat to HIGH and cook 2 minutes, or until sauce is slightly thickened, stirring occasionally. Serve over hot rice.

Did You Know?

This is the perfect recipe to put together when you get home from work, but before you go to Open House at school or your child's soccer practice. When you get back home, dinner will be ready to go!

SLOW COOKER

Roasted Garlic Chicken

Serves 4

- 6 tablespoons olive oil, divided
- 1 (3-pound) chicken, cut into 8 pieces
- 1 tablespoon finely chopped rosemary
- 1 teaspoon salt
- ½ teaspoon black pepper
- 1 head garlic, separated into cloves

1. In a skillet over medium heat, heat 2 tablespoons oil until hot. Brown half the chicken pieces on each side 3 to 5 minutes, turning once. Remove, add 2 tablespoons oil, and brown remaining chicken. Place chicken into a 6-quart or larger slow cooker.

2. In a small bowl, combine remaining oil, the rosemary, salt, and pepper. Brush over chicken and add garlic cloves.

3. Cover and cook on LOW 7 to 9 hours or on HIGH 3 to 4 hours, or until chicken is cooked through. (If cooking on HIGH add ½ cup of water)

Did You Know?

Garlic helps our bodies digest all sorts of foods and helps keep our glycemic index in check. All that, plus it tastes really good!

Chicken Mexicali

Serves 4

- 6 boneless, skinless chicken thighs, cut into 1-inch pieces
- 1 cup chicken broth
- 1 (14-½-ounce) can diced tomatoes with green chilies, undrained
- 1 (15-ounce) can black beans, rinsed and drained
- 1 cup chopped onion
- 1 cup frozen corn
- 1 tablespoon chili powder
- 1 teaspoon cumin
- 1 teaspoon salt
- 4 cups cooked yellow rice, warmed

1. Coat a 4-quart or larger slow cooker with cooking spray. Add all ingredients, except rice, and stir well to combine.

2. Cover and cook on HIGH 3 to 4 hours, or until chicken is cooked through and fork-tender. Spoon over rice and serve.

Serving Suggestion:
To take this over the top, how about finishing each serving off with dollops of sour cream, shredded cheese, and some diced avocado. It doesn't get any better than that!

Mediterranean Chicken Rollups

Serves 4

- 10 butter-flavored crackers
- 1 teaspoon butter, melted
- ¼ cup sun-dried tomatoes
- ½ cup olive oil
- 2 tablespoons fresh parsley, stems removed
- 2 cloves garlic
- 1 teaspoon salt, divided
- 1 teaspoon black pepper, divided
- 4 boneless, skinless chicken breast cutlets
- 4 ounces goat cheese, sliced into 4 pieces
- 4 large fresh basil leaves

1. In a resealable plastic bag, crush crackers; add butter, mix, and set aside.
2. In a blender or food processor, combine sun-dried tomatoes, oil, parsley, garlic, 1/4 teaspoon salt, and 1/4 teaspoon pepper; process until tomatoes are finely chopped.
3. Place chicken on a cutting board. Sprinkle both sides with remaining salt and pepper. Place one piece of goat cheese on each cutlet. Top each with a basil leaf, and a tablespoon of the sun-dried tomato mixture.
4. Roll up chicken and place seam-side down in a 4-quart or larger slow cooker. Spoon remaining sun-dried tomato mixture evenly over chicken and sprinkle with cracker topping.
5. Cover and cook on LOW 4-½ to 5 hours or on HIGH 2-½ to 3 hours, or until no pink remains.

Did You Know?

Cooking in a slow cooker not only allows you to have the freedom to do what you have to do while dinner is cooking, it also makes chicken dishes like this one really juicy through and through.

Chicken Stroganoff

Serves 4

- 2 tablespoons butter
- 4 boneless, skinless chicken breasts
- 1 (.7-ounce) package dry Italian-style salad dressing mix
- 1 (10.75-ounce) can condensed cream of mushroom soup
- ½ cup white wine or chicken broth
- 1 (8-ounce) package cream cheese, softened and cut into 2-inch pieces
- ¼ teaspoon black pepper
- 2 cups sliced fresh mushrooms
- Paprika for sprinkling

1. In a 5-quart or larger slow cooker, heat butter until melted. Evenly sprinkle both sides of the chicken with half the Italian dressing mix; place in slow cooker over butter.

2. In a large bowl, combine mushroom soup, wine, cream cheese, black pepper, and remaining Italian dressing mix until well-mixed. Stir in mushrooms and spoon over chicken. Sprinkle with paprika.

3. Cover and cook on LOW 4 to 5 hours or on HIGH 2 to 2-½ hours, or until chicken is no longer pink in the center.

Serving Suggestion:
Don't let your chicken be lonely! Team it up with some cooked egg noodles so they can soak up all that saucy goodness

Chicken Divan Casserole

Serves 6

- 1-½ pounds boneless, skinless chicken breasts, cut into 1-inch chunks
- 1 pound chopped fresh broccoli
- 1 (10.75-ounce) can cream of chicken soup
- ⅓ cup milk
- 2 cups shredded Cheddar cheese, divided
- ½ cup sour cream
- 1 teaspoon garlic powder
- ½ teaspoon dried thyme
- ½ teaspoon salt
- ¼ teaspoon black pepper
- 1 tablespoon butter, melted
- ¼ cup bread crumbs

1. In a 4-quart or larger slow cooker, place chicken, broccoli, soup, milk, 1 cup cheese, the sour cream, garlic powder, thyme, salt, and black pepper; stir well to combine.
2. Cover and cook on LOW 6 to 8 hours or on HIGH 3 to 4 hours, or until cooked through.
3. Sprinkle with remaining cheese. In a small bowl, mix butter and bread crumbs and sprinkle over cheese. Cover and cook on LOW 30 more minutes, or until cheese is melted. Serve immediately.

Test Kitchen · Mr. Food · Hints & Tips

Although chicken divan is most commonly made with chicken breasts like we do here, we also tested this with chicken thighs and we think it turned out even juicier. Ok, we'll admit it...we love dark meat chicken, but the choice is yours.

Tropical Lime Chicken

Serves 6

- 12 chicken thighs, skin removed
- ⅓ cup lime juice
- 1-½ cups chicken broth
- 4 cloves garlic, finely chopped
- 1 teaspoon dried thyme
- ½ teaspoon salt
- ¼ teaspoon black pepper
- 1 tablespoon butter
- 2 tablespoons cornstarch
- 2 tablespoons water
- 2 tablespoons chopped fresh parsley

1. In a 4-quart or larger slow cooker, combine chicken, lime juice, broth, garlic, thyme, salt, and pepper.
2. Cover and cook on LOW 5 to 6 hours or on HIGH 2 to 2-½ hours, or until chicken is no longer pink in center. Remove chicken to a platter.
3. Set slow cooker on HIGH. Add butter to broth mixture and stir until melted. In a small bowl, mix cornstarch and water. Whisk into broth mixture until thickened. Stir in parsley and add chicken back into sauce. Heat just until chicken is warmed, then serve topped with sauce.

If you want to get a jump start on this, you can make the sauce the night before but don't add the chicken to it until you are ready to cook. If you did, the acid in the lime juice would actually start to cook the chicken and make it rubbery.

Herbed Chicken & Orzo

Serves 4

- 2 red bell peppers, cut into 1-inch pieces
- 1 cup chopped onion
- 8 boneless, skinless chicken thighs, cut into 1-inch pieces
- 2 teaspoons dried oregano
- ½ teaspoon dried rosemary
- 1 teaspoon garlic powder
- 1 teaspoon salt, divided
- ½ teaspoon black pepper, divided
- 8 ounces uncooked orzo pasta
- ¼ cup lemon juice
- 1 cup chicken broth

1. Coat a 5-quart or larger slow cooker with cooking spray. Place bell pepper and onion in the bottom. Sprinkle chicken with oregano, rosemary, garlic powder, ¼ teaspoon salt, and ⅛ teaspoon black pepper. Place over peppers and onions.

2. Cover and cook on LOW 4 hours or on HIGH 2 hours (if cooking on HIGH, add ½ cup of the chicken broth now), or until chicken is no longer pink in center.

3. On HIGH add orzo, lemon juice, remaining broth, remaining salt, and remaining pepper. Stir, then cover and cook 30 to 45 more minutes, or until orzo is tender.

Did You Know?

Fresh herbs are less potent than dried. If you would like to use fresh herbs in place of the dried ones you will need to add 1 tablespoon of fresh in place of every teaspoon of dried.

Shortcut Chicken 'n' Dumplings

Serves 4

- 2 cups shredded rotisserie chicken
- 2 (10-¾-ounce) cans condensed cream of chicken soup, undiluted
- 2 cups water
- 2 cups frozen mixed vegetables
- 1 tablespoon all-purpose flour
- ½ teaspoon black pepper
- 1 (16.3-ounce) package refrigerated buttermilk biscuits (8 biscuits), quartered

1. In a 4-quart or larger slow cooker, mix all ingredients except biscuits. Gently fold in biscuit pieces.
2. Cover and cook on LOW 4 hours or on HIGH 2 hours, or until biscuits are cooked through, then serve.

Did You Know?

What makes this recipe so easy is that we can take advantage of so many of our market shortcuts. The chicken is pre-cooked, the frozen veggies are farm-fresh cleaned and cut, and the refrigerated biscuit dough is ready to use. Can't get easier than that!

Greek Stuffed Chicken Breasts

Serves 4

- 4 boneless, skinless chicken breasts, pounded to about ⅓-inch thick
- ¼ teaspoon salt
- ⅛ teaspoon black pepper
- ½ cup fresh spinach
- ½ cup sliced roasted red peppers, drained
- 1 (2.25-ounce) can sliced black olives, drained
- ¼ teaspoon dried oregano
- 1 cup chicken broth
- ¼ cup water
- 1 tablespoon cornstarch
- ½ cup crumbled feta cheese

1. Sprinkle both sides of chicken with salt and pepper. Place chicken on a cutting board and evenly top with layers of spinach, roasted peppers, and olives; sprinkle with oregano. Roll up jellyroll-style and secure each with a toothpick. Place in a 5-quart or larger pressure cooker; add chicken broth.

2. Securely lock lid and over high heat, bring to full pressure; reduce heat just enough to maintain pressure for 7 minutes. Perform a quick release. Remove chicken to a plate and cover to keep warm.

3. In a small bowl, whisk water and cornstarch until smooth. Over medium heat, whisk mixture into liquid in pressure cooker and simmer 1 to 2 minutes, or until thickened. Serve chicken topped with sauce and sprinkled with crumbled feta.

If using an electric pressure cooker prepare as directed above except:

- In step 2, set timer for 7 minutes.
- In step 3, simmer according to manufacturer's directions for your model.

For more details about how to use an electric pressure cooker, see pages xv-xvi.

15-Minute Chicken Cacciatore

Serves 4

- 1 (3-½-pound) chicken, cut into 8 pieces
- 1-½ teaspoons salt, divided
- 1 teaspoon black pepper, divided
- 1 (28-ounce) can diced tomatoes, undrained
- 8 ounces fresh mushrooms, quartered
- 1 large green bell pepper, cut into 1-inch chunks
- 1 large onion, chopped
- 3 cloves garlic, minced
- 1 (24-ounce) jar spaghetti sauce
- 2 teaspoons Italian seasoning

1 Sprinkle chicken with ½ teaspoon salt and ½ teaspoon pepper. Place in a 5-quart or larger pressure cooker. Add remaining ingredients over chicken in order listed. Do not stir.

2 Securely lock lid and over high heat, bring to full pressure; reduce just enough to maintain pressure for 12 minutes. Perform a quick release. Remove lid, stir, and serve chicken topped with sauce

Serving Suggestion:
How about topping this with some slivered basil and freshly grated Parmesan cheese? Hey...stop drooling and start cooking!

If using an electric pressure cooker prepare as directed above except:

- In step 2 set timer for 12 minutes.

For more details about how to use an electric pressure cooker, see pages xv-xvi.

Farm-Style Chicken with Biscuits

Serves 8

- 1 onion, chopped
- 1 celery stalk, cut into ½-inch slices
- 1 cup sliced fresh carrots
- 2 cups frozen peas
- 2 cups frozen corn
- 1-¼ pounds boneless, skinless chicken breasts, cut into 1-inch chunks
- 2 (12-ounce) jars chicken gravy, divided
- ½ cup water
- ¾ teaspoon salt
- ¼ teaspoon black pepper
- 1 (16.3-ounce) package refrigerated biscuits (8 biscuits)

1. Place onion, celery, carrots, peas, corn, chicken, 1 jar gravy, the water, salt, and pepper into a 6-quart or larger pressure cooker; stir.

2. Securely lock lid and over high heat, bring to full pressure; reduce heat just enough to maintain pressure for 8 minutes. Perform a quick release.

3. Meanwhile, bake biscuits according to package directions.

4. Stir remaining jar of gravy into chicken mixture and simmer until hot. Split biscuits in half and spoon chicken and gravy over each biscuit bottom. Place the top on and spoon more of the mixture over top.

Food for Thought:
Think of this dish as a "deconstructed" chicken pot pie. It has all the same flavors, without all the work. Now that's our idea of a quick dinner!

If using an electric pressure cooker prepare as directed above except:

- In step 2, set timer for 8 minutes.
- In step 4, simmer according to manufacturer's directions for your model.

For more details about how to use an electric pressure cooker, see pages xv-xvi.

Weeknight Chicken Marsala

PRESSURE COOKER

Serves 4

- 1/4 cup all-purpose flour
- 1/2 teaspoon salt
- 1/4 teaspoon black pepper
- 4 boneless, skinless chicken breasts
- 2 tablespoons butter
- 2 tablespoons vegetable oil
- 1/2 pound fresh mushrooms, cut in half
- 3/4 cup plus 2 tablespoons Marsala wine, divided
- 1 tablespoon cornstarch

1. In a shallow dish, combine flour, salt, and pepper. Evenly coat chicken with flour mixture. In a 4-1/2 quart or larger pressure cooker over medium heat, heat butter and oil. Sauté chicken 5 to 7 minutes, or until golden, turning halfway through. Add mushrooms and 3/4 cup Marsala wine to pressure cooker.

2. Securely lock lid and over high heat, bring to full pressure; reduce heat just enough to maintain pressure for 8 minutes. Perform a quick release. Remove chicken to a platter and cover to keep warm.

3. In a small bowl, combine remaining wine with cornstarch. Heat pan drippings with mushrooms in pressure cooker over high heat and slowly whisk in cornstarch mixture until thickened. Spoon sauce and mushrooms over chicken and serve.

Did You Know?

When cooking in a pressure cooker, all the flavors in the cooking liquid are infused into whatever you are cooking. Do you know what that means for you? Here it means that the rich flavor of the Marsala wine is going to be in every bite of chicken.

If using an electric pressure cooker prepare as directed above except:

- In step 1, sauté according to manufacturer's directions for your model.
- In step 2, set timer for 8 minutes.
- In step 3, heat according to manufacturer's directions for your model.

For more details about how to use an electric pressure cooker, see pages xv-xvi.

Chicken under Pressure

Serves 4

1 teaspoon paprika
¼ teaspoon dried thyme
¼ teaspoon poultry seasoning
½ teaspoon salt
¼ teaspoon black pepper
1 (3- to 3-½-pound) chicken
2 tablespoons olive oil
1-½ cups chicken broth
3 tablespoons lemon juice
2 tablespoons dry white wine (optional)
1 teaspoon browning and seasoning sauce
2 tablespoons cornstarch
¼ cup water
1 tablespoon chopped fresh parsley

1. In a small bowl, combine paprika, thyme, poultry seasoning, salt, and pepper. Rub mixture over chicken.
2. In a 5-quart or larger pressure cooker over medium heat, heat oil; sauté chicken, breast side down, and cook about 5 minutes, or until browned. Add chicken broth, lemon juice and wine, if desired.
3. Securely lock lid and over high heat, bring to full pressure; reduce heat just enough to maintain pressure for 25 minutes. Perform a natural release. Remove chicken from cooker and let rest 5 minutes.
4. Meanwhile, in a small bowl combine browning and seasoning sauce, cornstarch, and water. Slowly whisk into the pan drippings and simmer 3 to 5 minutes or until thickened; stir in parsley. Cut up chicken and serve with sauce.

If using an electric pressure cooker prepare as directed above except:

- In step 2, sauté according to manufacturer's directions for your model.
- In step 3, set timer for 25 minutes.
- In step 4, simmer according to manufacturer's directions for your model.

For more details about how to use an electric pressure cooker, see pages xv-xvi.

Twin Stuffed Cornish Hens

Serves 2

- 2 cups stuffing mix
- 1 cup hot water
- 1 tablespoon butter
- 2 Cornish hens (about 1-½ pounds each), thawed, if frozen
- 1 teaspoon onion powder
- 1 teaspoon salt
- ½ teaspoon black pepper
- 1 cup water
- 4 carrots, cut into 2-inch pieces
- ½ cup orange marmalade, melted

1. In a large bowl, mix together the stuffing mix, hot water, and butter until moistened. Place half the prepared stuffing in each hen. Sprinkle onion powder, salt, and pepper evenly over hens. In a 6-quart or larger pressure cooker add the water, and carrots; place hens over carrots.

2. Securely lock lid and over high heat, bring to full pressure; reduce heat just enough to maintain pressure for 8 minutes. Perform a natural release.

3. Preheat broiler. Place hens on a baking sheet; brush with marmalade.

4. Broil 3 to 5 minutes, or until glaze is caramelized and golden. **(Keep an eye on these so they don't burn.)**

If using an electric pressure cooker prepare as directed above except:

- In step 2, set timer for 8 minutes.

For more details about how to use an electric pressure cooker, see pages xv-xvi.

Thanksgiving Anytime Turkey Breast

Serves 6

- 1 teaspoon paprika
- 1 teaspoon poultry seasoning
- ½ teaspoon salt
- ¼ teaspoon black pepper
- 2 tablespoons vegetable oil
- 1 (6 to 7-pound) bone-in, skin-on turkey breast
- 1-¾ cups chicken broth
- 1 large onion, finely diced
- 1 celery stalk, diced
- 2 tablespoons cornstarch
- 4 tablespoons cold water
- 1 drop browning and seasoning sauce

1. In a small bowl, combine paprika, poultry seasoning, salt, pepper, and oil. Rub turkey with mixture. Place a trivet or foil collar (see page xiii) in bottom of 6-quart or larger pressure cooker. Add chicken broth, onion, and celery. Place turkey breast, skin side up, into cooker.
2. Securely lock lid and over high heat, bring to full pressure; reduce heat just enough to maintain pressure for 25 minutes. Perform a natural release.
3. Turkey should be 165°. If not, put lid on loosely and continue cooking on medium-low until it reaches 165°. Carefully remove turkey and place on serving platter. Cover with foil to keep warm.
4. Remove trivet or foil collar. In a small bowl, whisk together remaining ingredients; whisk into pan drippings and simmer until gravy thickens. Carve turkey and serve with gravy.

If using an electric pressure cooker prepare as directed above except:

- In step 2, set timer for 25 minutes.
- In step 3, if necessary, put lid on loosely and set timer for a few more minutes.
- In step 4, simmer according to manufacturer's directions for your model.

For more details about how to use an electric pressure cooker, see pages xv-xvi.

For All the Meat Lovers

Balsamic-Braised Short Ribs

Serves 4

- 3 pounds beef short ribs
- 1-½ tablespoons kosher salt
- 1-½ tablespoons black pepper
- 1-½ tablespoons olive oil
- 2 celery stalks, cut into ½-inch slices
- 2 carrots, cut into ½-inch slices
- 1 large onion, sliced
- 3 cloves garlic, minced
- 1 bay leaf
- 1 (14.5-ounce) can diced tomatoes, undrained
- ⅓ cup balsamic vinegar

1. Sprinkle short ribs with salt and pepper. In a large skillet, heat oil over medium-high heat. Add ribs and cook 2 to 3 minutes per side, or until just browned.
2. Place ribs in a 5-quart or larger slow cooker, fat side up. Top with remaining ingredients; toss gently to coat.
3. Cover and cook on LOW 7 to 8 hours or on HIGH 3-½ to 4 hours, or until meat is fall-apart tender.
4. Remove ribs and sauce to a serving platter, discard bay leaf, and serve.

Ginger Beef with Chinese Veggies

Serves 6

- 2 tablespoons vegetable oil
- 1 (1-½-pound) boneless beef chuck roast, cut into 1-inch chunks
- 2 onions, cut into ½-inch slices
- 6 cloves garlic, slivered
- 1 cup beef broth
- ½ cup water
- ¼ cup soy sauce
- 2 teaspoons ground ginger
- ⅛ teaspoon crushed red pepper (optional)
- 3 cups coarsely chopped bok choy
- 1 red bell pepper, cut into strips
- 1 (8-ounce) can bamboo shoots, drained

1. In a large skillet over medium-high heat, heat oil. Sauté beef, onions, and garlic until they begin to brown. Transfer to a 5-quart or larger slow cooker. Add broth, water, soy sauce, ginger, and crushed red pepper, if desired. Stir to combine.
2. Cover and cook on LOW 6 hours or on HIGH 3 to 4 hours, or until beef is tender.
3. Stir in bok choy, bell pepper, and bamboo shoots. Heat on HIGH 30 to 45 minutes, or until bok choy is tender.

Serving Suggestion:

This is amazing over rice! As for the type of rice, feel free to use anything from the more fragrant and flavorful jasmine or basmati, to a healthier brown rice option. Of course, if you're really pressed for time, the pre-cooked bagged rices, or a quick-cooking instant rice are always welcome.

Mom's No-Fuss Pot Roast

SLOW COOKER

Serves 8

- 3- to 4 pound boneless beef chuck roast, tied
- 1-½ teaspoons salt
- 1 teaspoon black pepper
- 1 teaspoon garlic powder
- 1 teaspoon onion powder
- 1 large onion, sliced
- ¼ cup all-purpose flour
- ¾ cup cold water

1. Sprinkle roast on all sides with salt, pepper, garlic powder, and onion powder. In a 4-½-quart or larger slow cooker, place roast with onions over the top.
2. Cover and cook on LOW 8 to 10 hours or on HIGH 6 to 7 hours, or until meat is tender. Remove roast to a cutting board and cover to keep warm.
3. In a small bowl, whisk together flour and water. Over high heat, slowly whisk into pan drippings until smooth; bring to a boil for 5 minutes, or until thickened.
4. Slice roast across the grain and serve up with the rich onion gravy.

If using a frozen roast, yes, you can use a frozen one...make sure you add an additional hour to the cooking time.

Creamy Beef Stroganoff

Serves 4

- 1 (10-3/4-ounce) can condensed cream of mushroom soup
- 3 tablespoons water
- 2 tablespoons Worcestershire sauce
- 8 ounces sliced mushrooms
- 1 onion, coarsely chopped
- 2 cloves garlic, minced
- 1/4 teaspoon salt
- 1/4 teaspoon black pepper
- 1-1/2 pounds beef stew meat, well-trimmed
- 1/2 cup sour cream
- 8 ounces medium egg noodles, cooked and drained

1. In a 6-quart or larger slow cooker, stir soup, water, Worcestershire sauce, mushrooms, onion, garlic, salt, and black pepper. Add the beef and stir to coat.

2. Cover and cook on LOW 6 to 7 hours, or until beef is fork tender. Stir in sour cream and serve over warmed noodles.

If you don't see beef stew meat in the meat case, no problem. Simply pick up a bottom round steak and cut it into 1-inch chunks.

Weeknight Steak Fajitas

Serves 4

- 1 (1-pound) flank steak, thinly sliced
- 1 onion, cut in half and sliced
- ½ cup salsa
- 2 tablespoons lime juice
- 3 tablespoons chopped fresh cilantro
- 2 cloves garlic, minced
- 1 tablespoon chili powder
- 1 teaspoon ground cumin
- ½ teaspoon salt
- 1 red bell pepper, cut into strips
- 1 green bell pepper, cut into strips
- 8 (6-inch) flour tortillas
- 1 cup (4 ounces) shredded Cheddar cheese

1. In a 5-quart or larger slow cooker, add meat, onion, salsa, lime juice, cilantro, garlic, chili powder, cumin, and salt. Toss to coat.

2. Cover and cook on LOW 4 hours, or until fork-tender. Add bell peppers. Cover and cook on LOW another 45 minutes.

3. Place on a serving platter and serve with warmed tortillas and Cheddar cheese.

Just in case you're thinking, "Is there any easy way to cut the steak into thin slices while it's still raw?" The answer is yes! Simply place the steak in the freezer for about 15 minutes to firm up, and then slice it across the grain. Yup, that's how it's done. (Or you could always ask your butcher to do it for you.)

Salt-Crusted Roast Beef

SLOW COOKER

Serves 8

- 1/3 cup vegetable oil
- 1 small onion, finely chopped
- 2 cloves garlic, minced
- 1 (2-1/2 to 3 pound) beef eye of round roast, trimmed
- 4 cups kosher salt
- 2 tablespoons black pepper
- 1 cup water

1. In a large resealable plastic bag, combine oil, onion, and garlic; close tightly and shake to mix well. Place roast in bag, seal, and turn to coat completely with mixture. Marinate in refrigerator at least 2 hours or overnight.

2. Line a 4-1/2 quart or larger slow cooker with heavy-duty aluminum foil. In a medium bowl, combine salt, pepper, and water; mix well. Place half the mixture on center of foil. Place roast on top of mixture then coat with remaining salt mixture, completely coating roast, forming a crust about 1/2-inch thick. Loosely cover with foil.

3. Cover and cook on LOW 8 to 10 hours or on HIGH 4 to 5 hours.

4. Using foil, carefully lift roast out of slow cooker to a cutting board. Remove and discard salt crust. Slice roast across the grain and serve immediately.

Food for Thought:

The salt crust creates a jacket around the roast and seals in its juices and natural goodness. What you end up with is lots of flavor without it being salty. Really, it's delicious.

Ready and Waiting Goulash

Serves 6

- 2 pounds top round beef, cut into 1-inch pieces
- 1 cup chopped onion
- 3 cloves garlic, minced
- 2 tablespoons all-purpose flour
- 1 tablespoon paprika
- 1 teaspoon salt
- ½ teaspoon black pepper
- 1 teaspoon dried thyme
- 1 (28-ounce) can diced tomatoes, undrained
- 3 carrots, cut into 1-½-inch chunks
- 1 bay leaf
- 1 (8-ounce) container sour cream

1. In a 4-½ quart or larger slow cooker, combine steak, onion, and garlic.
2. In a small bowl, combine flour, paprika, salt, pepper, and thyme; mix well. Add to meat mixture, tossing to coat. Add tomatoes with liquid, carrots, and bay leaf; mix well.
3. Cover and cook on LOW 8 to 9 hours or on HIGH 4-½ to 5 hours, or until beef is fork-tender. Discard bay leaf. Stir in sour cream and serve.

Serving Suggestion:

Serve this up over warm buttered noodles and watch the gang come running.

Orzo-Stuffed Peppers

Serves 6

- 1 pound ground beef
- ½ pound bulk Italian sausage
- 1 cup uncooked orzo pasta
- 1 (29-ounce) can tomato sauce, divided
- ½ teaspoon dried basil
- 1 teaspoon garlic powder
- 1 teaspoon salt
- ½ teaspoon black pepper
- 6 bell peppers (any color), tops removed and cored
- ½ cup water

1. In a large bowl, combine ground beef, sausage, orzo, 1-½ cups tomato sauce, the basil, garlic powder, salt, and pepper; mix well. Stuff bell peppers evenly with mixture.

2. Stand peppers in a 6-quart or larger slow cooker and pour remaining tomato sauce over top. Pour water in bottom of slow cooker.

3. Cook on LOW 7 to 8 hours or on HIGH 3-½ to 4 hours, or until meat and pasta are thoroughly cooked and peppers are tender.

Did You Know?

Slow cookers sure have come a long way! Now, beyond the traditional sizes and shapes, you can even find them rectangular, which makes them perfect for casseroles and dishes like this.

Easy French Dip Sandwiches

Serves 8

- 1 (4-pound) beef rump roast, trimmed
- 1 (10.5-ounce) can beef broth
- 1 (10.5-ounce) can condensed French onion soup
- 1 (12-ounce) can or bottle beer
- 8 French rolls
- 16 slices mozzarella cheese

1. In a 6-quart or larger slow cooker, place roast. Add broth, onion soup, and beer.
2. Cover and cook on LOW 7 hours, or until meat is fork-tender. Carefully remove roast from slow cooker, reserving gravy, and place on a cutting board; shred with 2 forks.
3. Preheat oven to 350° F. Cut each roll in half, but not all the way through, and place on a baking sheet. Place a slice of cheese on each roll, top with shredded beef and another slice of cheese.
4. Bake 3 to 5 minutes, or until cheese is melted. Serve with a bowl of the gravy for dipping.

The key to shredding the beef is to make sure the beef is cooked to what we call "fall-apart tender." Then, simply use two forks and pull or shred the meat so it becomes thin strands of tender yumminess.

Grandma's Best Brisket

Serves 6

- 1 (4-½-pound) beef brisket
- 1 teaspoon salt
- ½ teaspoon black pepper
- 1 (10.5-ounce) can condensed beef broth
- 1 (10.5-ounce) can French onion soup
- 1 large onion, thinly sliced
- 6 creamer potatoes, cut in half
- 1 (8-ounce) bag baby carrots

1. Sprinkle both sides of brisket with salt and pepper. Place in a 6-quart or larger slow cooker, fat side up. Add remaining ingredients.

2. Cover, and cook on LOW for 7 to 8 hours or on HIGH 4 to 5 hours.

3. Remove brisket to a cutting board and allow to rest 5 minutes. Slice across the grain and serve with the vegetables and the gravy.

The reason you should always place a roast fat side up when cooking is that while it cooks and the fat melts away, it self-bastes the rest of the roast. The results are juicier meat with lots of flavor. Grandma was one smart cookie!

Topless Reubens

Serves 6

- 1 (2-½-pound) corned beef brisket with pickling spices, trimmed
- 1 onion, sliced
- 1 cup water
- 3 cups sauerkraut, drained
- 6 slices rye bread
- 12 slices Swiss cheese
- ½ cup Russian dressing

1. Place corned beef in a 5-quart or larger slow cooker, fat side up. Sprinkle with pickling spice packet. Top with onion and water.
2. Cover and cook on LOW 7 to 8 hours, or until fork-tender. Add sauerkraut and cook another hour. Remove beef from slow cooker to a cutting board and slice thinly across the grain.
3. Preheat oven to 400° F. Place bread slices on a baking sheet. Spread each slice with Russian dressing. Top evenly with sauerkraut. Pile meat evenly on each sandwich, then place 2 slices of cheese on top.
4. Bake 5 minutes, or until cheese is melted. Serve immediately.

Food for Thought:
If you're used to buying your corned beef sliced from the deli, you're in for a real treat when you make it at home and slice it yourself.

Rancher's Meatloaf

Serves 6

2 pounds ground chuck

¾ cup barbecue sauce, divided

½ cup chopped onion

½ cup Italian-seasoned dry bread crumbs

1 large egg

½ teaspoon salt

¼ teaspoon black pepper

1. Coat a 5-quart or larger slow cooker with cooking spray.
2. In a large bowl, combine meat, ½ cup barbecue sauce, the onion, bread crumbs, egg, salt, and pepper; mix well, but do not over-mix as it will make the meatloaf tough.
3. Shape mixture into a loaf and place in slow cooker. Spread remaining barbecue sauce over loaf.
4. Cook on LOW 6 to 6-½ hours or on HIGH 3 to 3-½ hours, or until no longer pink in center. Cut into thick slices and serve.

Food for Thought:

The reason we suggest ground chuck for this recipe is that it typically has a higher fat content which keeps our meatloaf nice and moist. Basically, we recommend an 80/20 blend.

Smothered Pork Chops

Serves 6

- 5 slices bacon, cooked and crumbled, drippings reserved
- 6 (3⁄4-inch-thick) bone-in pork loin chops, patted dry
- 1⁄2 teaspoon salt, divided
- 1⁄4 teaspoon black pepper
- 2 onions, cut into half-moon slices
- 2 tablespoon light brown sugar, divided
- 1⁄4 cup plus 2 tablespoons cold water, divided
- 3 cloves garlic, minced
- 1 teaspoon dried thyme
- 2 cups chicken broth
- 1 tablespoon soy sauce
- 1 tablespoon cornstarch

1. In a large skillet over medium heat, heat bacon drippings until hot. Season pork chops with 1/4 teaspoon salt and the pepper, then cook in batches until golden. Place them in a 6-quart or larger slow cooker. Reserve 1 tablespoon pan drippings in skillet.

2. In skillet, add onions, 1 tablespoon brown sugar, the remaining salt, and 1/4 cup water. Cook over medium-high heat, making sure to scrape the brown bits from the bottom of the pan with a wooden spoon. Cook 4 to 5 minutes, or until onions are soft. Stir in garlic and thyme and cook about 30 seconds. Add onion mixture, broth, and soy sauce to slow cooker.

3. Cover and cook on LOW about 6 hours or on HIGH about 3 hours, or until pork is tender. Remove chops and onions to a serving platter; loosely cover with foil to keep warm.

4. In a small bowl, whisk cornstarch and remaining water, then slowly whisk into slow cooker. On high heat, cook 3 to 5 minutes, or until thickened. Stir in crumbled bacon and serve over pork chops.

Cranberry-Glazed Stuffed Pork Roast

Serves 4

- 1 (6-ounce) package pork stuffing mix
- ½ cup dried cranberries
- 1 (2 to 2-½ pound) boneless pork loin
- ¾ teaspoon salt, divided
- ¼ cup black pepper
- ⅓ cup orange marmalade
- ½ cup dried cranberries
- 1 (14-ounce) can whole berry cranberry sauce
- 2 tablespoons chopped fresh parsley

1. Prepare stuffing mix according to package directions. Stir in cranberries; set aside.
2. Place pork loin on a cutting board and cut 4 deep horizontal slits across the roast. Season with ½ teaspoon salt and the pepper. Equally fill each opening with stuffing and place into slow cooker, stuffing side up.
3. In a bowl, combine remaining ingredients; mix well. Pour half the cranberry mixture, and sprinkle with parsley.
4. Cover and cook on LOW 4 to 4-½ hours or until center of the pork is 140° and slightly pink. To serve, cut between the stuffing and meat, top with remaining cranberry mixture, and sprinkle with parsley.

Food for Thought:

You guessed it, this is beautiful enough to serve on any special occasion, yet easy enough to make any night of the week! Now that's what we call a double bonus.

Chinese-Style Pork

Serves 6

- 1 (3-pound) boneless pork butt
- ⅛ teaspoon plus ½ teaspoon salt, divided
- ⅛ teaspoon black pepper
- 2 bell peppers (one red, one green) cut into 1-½ inch chunks
- 1 large onion, chopped
- 2 cups sliced mushrooms
- 1 (10.5-ounce) can condensed beef broth
- 3 tablespoons soy sauce
- 1 tablespoon sesame oil
- 2 cloves garlic, minced
- 1 teaspoon five-spice powder
- 1 teaspoon ground ginger
- 2 tablespoon cornstarch
- 3 tablespoons water

1. Evenly sprinkle pork with ⅛ teaspoon salt and the pepper, and place in a 5-quart or larger slow cooker. Place bell peppers, onion, and mushrooms around the meat.

2. In a medium bowl, combine beef broth, soy sauce, sesame oil, garlic, five-spice powder, ginger, and remaining salt. Pour over meat.

3. Cover and cook on LOW 8 hours or on HIGH 5 hours, or until meat is fork-tender. Remove to a cutting board and shred using 2 forks.

4. In a small bowl, whisk together cornstarch and water then whisk into the slow cooker. Cook on HIGH until thickened, then return the meat to the sauce and mix well. Serve immediately or keep warm until ready to serve.

Serving Suggestion:

We got this recipe form a good friend of the Test Kitchen. After we tested it, we knew we had to include it in this book. Just make sure you serve it over some hot cooked white or brown rice and dinner is ready.

Mouthwatering Mushroom Pot Roast

Serves 6

- 1-½ cups beef broth
- 2 tablespoons tomato paste
- 1 (3-½-pound) beef chuck roast
- 2 tablespoons soy sauce
- Salt and pepper for sprinkling
- 1 onion, coarsely chopped
- 2 cloves garlic, slivered
- 8 ounces sliced mushrooms

1. In a 4-1/2 quart or larger pressure cooker, combine beef broth and tomato paste, stirring until well mixed. Place a foil collar or trivet (see page xiii) in the pressure cooker. Brush all sides of roast with soy sauce, then sprinkle with salt and pepper. Place meat on foil collar. Add remaining ingredients.

2. Securely lock lid and over high heat, bring to full pressure; reduce heat just enough to maintain pressure for 50 minutes. Perform a natural release.

3. Remove meat to a cutting board; carve into thick slices or cut into chunks. Serve with mushrooms and pan drippings

Brushing a roast before cooking in a pressure cooker gives it a rich caramel color when it's done, rather than looking gray and blah.

If using an electric pressure cooker prepare as directed above except:

- In Step 2, set timer for 50 minutes.

For more details about how to use an electric pressure cooker, see pages xv-xvi.

Fastest Corned Beef & Cabbage

Serves 4

- 1 (3-pound) uncooked corned beef with pickling spices and liquid
- 2-½ cups water, divided
- 1 large head cabbage, quartered
- 4 large carrots, cut into 3-inch chunks
- 6 potatoes, peeled and cut in half
- ½ teaspoon salt
- ¼ teaspoon black pepper

1. Place corned beef with pickling spices and liquid and 2 cups water in a 5-quart or larger pressure cooker.
2. Securely lock lid and over high heat, bring to full pressure; reduce heat just enough to maintain pressure for 60 minutes. Perform a quick release. Remove corned beef and place on a cutting board; cover to keep warm.
3. Add remaining water and remaining ingredients to pressure cooker. Securely lock lid and over high heat, bring to full pressure; reduce heat just enough to maintain pressure for 4 minutes. Perform a natural release.
4. With a slotted spoon, remove vegetables to a serving platter. Slice corned beef against grain and serve with vegetables

Food for Thought:

With how easy and tasty this is, you won't have to wait until St. Patrick's Day to serve it. You could make this any night of the week, and then use the leftovers in hash.

If using an electric pressure cooker prepare as directed above except:

- In step 2, set timer for 60 minutes.
- In step 3, set timer for 4 minutes.

For more details about how to use an electric pressure cooker, see pages xv-xvi.

Short Ribs with Barley

Serves 4

- 2 tablespoons vegetable oil
- 3-½ pounds beef short ribs
- 1 onion, chopped
- 8 small creamer potatoes
- 2 cups beef broth
- 1 cup water
- 2 tablespoons teriyaki sauce
- 2 teaspoons paprika
- 1 teaspoon salt
- ¼ teaspoon black pepper
- ½ cup barley

1. Heat oil in a pressure cooker over HIGH heat. Add short ribs and cook, uncovered, 8 to 10 minutes, or until browned on all sides. Add remaining ingredients.

2. Securely lock lid and over high heat, bring to full pressure; reduce heat just enough to maintain pressure for 12 minutes. Perform a natural release. Remove lid, stir, and serve these fall-off-the-bones short ribs with potatoes and barley.

Serving Suggestion:
The only thing missing with this is either a tossed salad or a green vegetable. We'll leave that up to you. Hmmm, all of life's decisions should be that simple!

If using an electric pressure cooker prepare as directed above except:

- In step 1, brown according to manufacturer's directions for your model.
- In step 2, set timer for 12 minutes.

For more details about how to use an electric pressure cooker, see pages xv-xvi.

Saucy Meatball Hoagies

Serves 4

1-½ pounds ground beef
¾ cup plain bread crumbs
½ cup grated Parmesan cheese
1 cup water, divided
¼ cup coarsely chopped fresh parsley
1 egg
2 teaspoons garlic powder
1 teaspoon salt
½ teaspoon black pepper
1 (24-ounce) jar spaghetti sauce
4 hoagie rolls, split and toasted

1. In a large bowl, gently combine beef, bread crumbs, cheese, ½ cup water, the parsley, egg, garlic powder, salt, and pepper (see Tip). Form mixture into 12 equal-sized meatballs and place in a 6-quart or larger pressure cooker. Add spaghetti sauce and remaining water, and stir gently to mix, being careful not to break up meatballs.

2. Securely lock lid and over high heat, bring to full pressure; reduce heat just enough to maintain pressure for 10 minutes. Perform a quick release.

3. Remove lid and stir. Spoon 3 meatballs, with sauce, on top of each toasted roll and serve immediately.

The key to plump, tender meatballs is not to over-mix, over-handle, or over-pack the meat mixture. Treat the ground beef with a little TLC and you'll end up with some of the best meatballs you've ever had.

If using an electric pressure cooker prepare as directed above except:

- In step 2, set timer for 10 minutes.

For more details about how to use an electric pressure cooker, see pages xv-xvi.

Cowboy Beef Brisket

Serves 5

- 1 tablespoon salt
- ½ teaspoon black pepper
- 2 teaspoons garlic powder
- 1 tablespoon paprika
- 1 (3- to 4-pound) beef brisket, trimmed
- ½ cup firmly packed brown sugar
- 2 tablespoons white vinegar
- 1 cup water
- ½ cup ketchup
- 1 teaspoon liquid smoke (optional)
- 1 onion, thinly sliced

1. In a 6-quart or larger pressure cooker, place a trivet or foil collar. (see page xiii)
2. In a small bowl, combine salt, pepper, garlic powder, and paprika. Rub mixture over brisket and place fat side up on trivet in pressure cooker.
3. In a bowl, combine brown sugar, vinegar, water, ketchup, and liquid smoke, if desired; pour over brisket. Lay onion slices on top of meat.
4. Securely lock lid and over high heat, bring to full pressure; reduce heat just enough to maintain pressure for 50 minutes. Perform a natural release.
5. Place brisket on a cutting board, slice against the grain, and serve with the barbecue sauce from the pressure cooker.

Did You Know?

The reason we use a trivet or a collar is because this cooks for quite some time, and the sauce contains ketchup and brown sugar. Raising the meat off the bottom will prevent it from scorching. See, just like mom said, there's a reason for everything.

If using an electric pressure cooker prepare as directed above except:

- In step 4, set timer for 50 minutes.

For more details about how to use an electric pressure cooker, see pages xv-xvi.

Tropical Pulled Pork Sliders

Serves 10

- 1 (2- to 3-pound) boneless pork shoulder roast
- 1 teaspoon salt
- ½ teaspoon black pepper
- 2 cups water
- 1 (28-ounce) bottle barbecue sauce
- 1 (8-ounce) can pineapple tidbits, undrained
- 10 slider rolls

1. Sprinkle roast with salt and pepper on both sides. Place trivet or foil collar (see page xiii) in 6-quart or larger pressure cooker; add water. Place pork on trivet.

2. Securely lock lid and over high heat, bring to full pressure; reduce heat just enough to maintain pressure for 75 minutes. Perform a natural release.

3. Remove pork to a cutting board and shred with 2 forks. Discard liquid from pressure cooker. Add barbecue sauce, pineapple, and shredded meat to cooker. Mix well, and over medium heat, simmer 5 minutes, or until heated through. Serve on slider rolls.

Serving Suggestion:

Whip up or buy a batch of your favorite cole slaw and top each slider with a spoonful of it. Yep, right on top of the pork!

If using an electric pressure cooker prepare as directed above except:

- In step 2, set timer for 75 minutes.
- In step 3, simmer according to manufacturer's directions for your model.

For more details about how to use an electric pressure cooker, see pages xv-xvi.

BBQ Raspberry-Glazed Ribs

Serves 4

- 1 teaspoon dried thyme
- 1 teaspoon garlic powder
- 1 teaspoon onion powder
- 1 teaspoon salt
- ½ teaspoon black pepper
- 5 pounds baby back pork ribs
- 1 cup barbecue sauce
- 1 (18-ounce) jar seedless red raspberry jam
- 1 cup Thai chili sauce

1. Preheat oven to broil. Coat a rimmed baking sheet with cooking spray. n a small bowl, combine thyme, garlic powder, onion powder, salt, and pepper. Rub mixture evenly over both sides of ribs and place on baking sheet.

2. Broil 3 to 5 minutes per side, or until browned. Let cool 5 minutes, then cut into 2-rib sections. Place in a 6-quart or larger pressure cooker.

3. In a medium bowl, combine barbecue sauce, raspberry jam, and chili sauce; mix well and pour over ribs.

4. Securely lock lid in place and over high heat, bring to full pressure; reduce heat just enough to maintain pressure for 30 minutes. Perform a natural release. Remove ribs and serve with sauce.

If using an electric pressure cooker prepare as directed above except:

- In step 4, set timer for 30 minutes.

For more details about how to use an electric pressure cooker, see pages xv-xvi.

South-of-the-Border Braised Pork

Serves 6

- 3 tablespoons vegetable oil
- 1 (3-pound) boneless pork shoulder, cut into 1-½-inch cubes
- 2 jalapeno peppers, roughly chopped (or more to taste)
- 1 large onion, roughly chopped
- 4 cloves garlic, roughly chopped
- 1 teaspoon coriander
- 3 tablespoons ground cumin
- 1 teaspoon chili powder
- ½ teaspoon salt
- ¼ teaspoon black pepper
- 1-½ cups beef broth

1. In a 6-quart or larger pressure cooker over medium-high heat, heat oil. Brown pork on all sides and stir in remaining ingredients.

2. Securely lock lid and over high heat, bring to full pressure; reduce heat just enough to maintain pressure for 10 minutes Perform a quick release. The pork should be fall-apart tender. If not, place lid on loosely, and simmer until it is, then serve

Serving Suggestion:
We served this with yellow rice, which was perfect since it soaked up all the pan drippings. After all, that's where lots of the flavor is.

If using an electric pressure cooker prepare as directed above except:

- In step 1, brown according to manufacturer's directions for your model.
- In step 2, set timer for 10 minutes.
- If necessary, simmer according to manufacturer's directions for your model.

For more details about how to use an electric pressure cooker, see pages xv-xvi.

Root Beer Pork

PRESSURE COOKER

Serves 6

- 1 teaspoon salt
- ½ teaspoon black pepper
- 1 teaspoon garlic powder
- 1 (3-pound) boneless pork butt or shoulder roast
- 2 tablespoons vegetable oil
- 1 (12-ounce) can root beer
- 2 (12-ounce) bottles chili sauce
- 2 tablespoons Worcestershire sauce
- 2 teaspoons hot pepper sauce
- 1 (8-inch) round corn bread, cut into wedges

1. In a small bowl, combine salt, pepper, and garlic powder. Rub mixture over meat.
2. In a large skillet over high heat, heat oil; brown pork on all sides.
3. Place a steamer insert or foil collar (see page xiii) in a 6-quart or larger pressure cooker. Place meat on insert. In a large bowl, combine remaining ingredients, except corn bread; pour over pork.
4. Securely lock lid and over high heat, bring to full pressure; reduce heat just enough to maintain pressure for 60 minutes. Perform a quick release. Check to ensure meat is very tender. If not, place lid on loosely and simmer until fork- tender. Remove meat to a cutting board and cut into chunks.
5. Skim fat from sauce and stir meat back into sauce. Serve over wedges of cornbread.

If using an electric pressure cooker prepare as directed above except:

- In step 4, set timer for 60 minutes.
- If necessary, simmer according to manufacturer's directions for your model.

For more details about how to use an electric pressure cooker, see pages xv-xvi.

Apple Sauerkraut Pork Chops

Serves 4

- 2 tablespoons vegetable oil
- 4 (3/4-inch-thick) pork loin chops (1 to 1-1/2 pounds total)
- 1/2 teaspoon salt
- 1/4 teaspoon black pepper
- 3 sweet potatoes (about 1-1/2 pounds), peeled and cut into 2-inch chunks
- 3 Granny Smith apples, peeled, cored, and cut in half
- 1/2 cup apple juice
- 1/2 cup firmly packed light brown sugar
- 2 teaspoons ground cinnamon
- 1 pound sauerkraut, drained, squeezed dry

1. In a 6-quart or larger pressure cooker over high heat, heat oil. Sprinkle pork chops with salt and pepper. Add 2 chops to pressure cooker and brown, uncovered, 4 to 6 minutes, turning halfway through cooking. Remove to a platter and repeat with remaining chops.
2. Place sweet potatoes in bottom of pressure cooker, then layer pork chops and apples on top.
3. In a small bowl, combine apple juice, brown sugar, and cinnamon; mix well and pour over pork chops. Top with sauerkraut.
4. Securely lock lid and over high heat, bring to full pressure; reduce heat just enough to maintain pressure for 9 minutes. Perform a quick release. Remove lid and serve.

If using an electric pressure cooker prepare as directed above except:

- In step 1, brown according to manufacturer's directions for your model.
- In step 4, set timer for 9 minutes.

For more details about how to use an electric pressure cooker, see pages xv-xvi.

Seafood, Pasta & More

Spinach Parmesan-Crusted Salmon

Serves 4

- 1 (14-ounce) can artichoke heart quarters, undrained
- 1 (1-½ pound) salmon fillet
- 1 (9-ounce) package frozen creamed spinach, thawed
- ¼ cup grated Parmesan cheese

1. In a 6-quart or larger slow cooker, layer the artichoke hearts in the bottom. Top with the salmon, tucking in the ends to fit. Spoon the creamed spinach over the salmon.
2. Cover and cook on HIGH 1-¼ to 1-½ hours, or until fish flakes easily with a fork. Sprinkle with Parmesan cheese and serve fish with artichokes.

We love cooking fish in a slow cooker, since it makes every bite super moist and flavorful. Plus, since this is all made in just one pot, clean-up is a breeze. Now that's the kind of cookin' we like!

Mediterranean Catfish

Serves 4

- 1 tablespoon olive oil
- ½ cup chopped red onion
- 2 cloves garlic, chopped
- 1 (14-½-ounce) can diced tomatoes, undrained
- 1 teaspoon dried oregano
- ½ teaspoon salt
- ½ teaspoon black pepper
- ¼ teaspoon hot sauce (optional)
- 4 (4-ounce) farm-raised catfish fillets
- ¼ cup sliced black olives, drained
- ¼ cup crumbled feta cheese

1. In a skillet over medium heat, heat oil. Sauté onion and garlic 3 to 5 minutes, or until tender. Add tomatoes, oregano, salt, pepper, and hot sauce, if desired; mix well.
2. Place half the tomato mixture in a 6-quart or larger slow cooker. Lay fish on top, tucking in ends to fit, if necessary. Spoon remaining tomato mixture over fish.
3. Cover and cook on HIGH 1 to 1-¼ hours, or until fillets flake easily with a fork. Garnish with olives and feta cheese, and serve.

As you may know, we love US farm-raised catfish here in the Test Kitchen. As a matter of fact, we always keep a bag or two in the freezer for whenever we feel like whipping up something quick and tasty.

Worry-Free Tuna Noodle Casserole

SLOW COOKER

Serves 6

- 2 (10-¾-ounce) cans condensed cream of mushroom soup
- 2 cups milk
- ½ cup water
- ½ teaspoon black pepper
- 1 (16-ounce) package uncooked rotini pasta
- 2 cups frozen peas
- 2 cups (8 ounces) shredded Swiss cheese, divided
- 1 (12-ounce) can tuna packed in water, drained, flaked

1. Coat a 5-quart or larger slow cooker with cooking spray.
2. In a large bowl, combine soup, milk, water, and pepper; mix well. Stir in pasta, peas, 1-½ cups Swiss cheese, and the tuna. Pour mixture into slow cooker.
3. Cover and cook on LOW 4 hours or on HIGH 2-½ hours, or until pasta is tender. Sprinkle remaining cheese over top during last 30 minutes of cooking. Serve immediately.

Did You Know?

Over the years we have made many versions of this popular favorite. They've had everything from crushed potato chips to fried onions on top. We purposely left those off of this version and topped it with more cheese, since we found that the moist heat in the slow cooker makes those toppings soggy.

Mile-High Veggie Lasagna

SLOW COOKER

Serves 6

- 2 (15-ounce) containers ricotta cheese
- 1 (10-ounce) package frozen chopped spinach, thawed, squeezed dry
- 1 cup shredded carrots
- 2 cups sliced mushrooms
- 1 cup shredded zucchini
- 2 tablespoons chopped basil
- ½ teaspoon salt
- ¼ teaspoon black pepper
- 4-½ cups shredded mozzarella cheese
- ½ cup grated Parmesan cheese
- 3 cups spaghetti sauce
- 8 to 10 lasagna noodles, uncooked (oven ready)

1. In a large bowl, combine ricotta cheese, spinach, carrots, mushrooms, zucchini, basil, salt, and pepper. In a medium bowl, combine the mozzarella and Parmesan cheeses.

2. In a 6-quart or larger slow cooker, spread about ½ cup sauce in a thin layer. Cover with a single layer of noodles, breaking them, as needed, to fit. Spread half the vegetable mixture over noodles. Top with about ⅓ of remaining sauce, then sprinkle with about ⅓ of mozzarella mixture. Repeat layers. Top with remaining noodles, then remaining sauce.

3. Cover and cook on LOW 3-½ hours. Sprinkle with remaining mozzarella cheese; cover and cook another 30 minutes. Uncover and let rest 15 minutes, so excess liquid is absorbed before serving.

Lighten it Up:

You can lighten this up by using both lighter ricotta and mozzarella cheeses. That, along with the fact that this is brimming with lots of veggies, makes this not only unbelievably tasty, but good for us, too!

Little Italy Baked Ziti

Serves 6

- 1-¼ pounds Italian bulk sausage
- 1 onion, chopped
- 2 cloves garlic, minced
- 1 (15-ounce) container ricotta cheese
- 1 egg, beaten
- 2-½ cups shredded mozzarella cheese, divided
- 1 cup Parmesan cheese, divided
- ½ teaspoon Italian seasoning
- 2 (24-ounce) jars spaghetti sauce
- 1 (16-ounce) box uncooked ziti pasta

1. Coat a 5-quart or larger slow cooker with cooking spray.
2. In a large skillet over medium-high heat, cook sausage, onion, and garlic 6 to 8 minutes, or until browned; drain and set aside.
3. In a medium bowl, combine ricotta cheese, egg, 1 cup mozzarella, ½ cup Parmesan, and the Italian seasoning; mix well.
4. Place 2 cups of sauce on the bottom of slow cooker. Top with half the sausage mixture, ½ cup mozzarella, half the ziti, and half the ricotta mixture. Repeat layers. Top with remaining sauce, and sprinkle with remaining Parmesan.
5. Cover and cook on LOW 4 to 5 hours or on HIGH 2-½ hours, or until pasta is tender, sprinkling with remaining mozzarella cheese during last 30 minutes of cooking.

Anytime Mac 'n' Cheese

Serves 6

- 1 (10-¾-ounce) can condensed Cheddar cheese soup
- 2 cups whole milk
- 2 sticks plus 2 tablespoons butter, melted, divided
- ½ teaspoon black pepper
- 4 cups shredded Cheddar cheese
- 1 cup shredded mozzarella cheese
- 1 (16-ounce) package uncooked elbow macaroni
- 1 cup coarsely crushed butter-flavored crackers

1. In a 4-quart or larger slow cooker, combine the soup, milk, 2 sticks butter, and the pepper. Stir in the Cheddar and mozzarella cheeses, and the macaroni.
2. In a small bowl, combine crackers and remaining butter. Sprinkle over macaroni and cheese mixture.
3. Cover and cook on LOW 3 hours or on HIGH 1-½ hours, or until pasta is tender and it's bubbling hot.

Patty, our Test Kitchen Director, prefers to cook this on HIGH heat. That's how you get that brown and crispy outside crust, which she swears is the best part.

Spoonable Pepperoni Pizza Bake

Serves 6

- 2-½ cups pancake and biscuit baking mix (like Bisquick)
- 1 cup water
- 1 (14-ounce) jar pizza sauce, plus more for topping (optional)
- 1 (4-ounce) package sliced pepperoni
- ½ pound Italian bulk sausage, cooked and crumbled
- 2 cups (8 ounces) shredded mozzarella cheese

1. Coat a 6-quart or larger slow cooker with cooking spray.
2. In a bowl, stir baking mix and water until soft dough forms. Drop ½ the dough by spoonfuls evenly into bottom of slow cooker. (Dough does not have to completely cover the bottom.)
3. Spoon 1 cup sauce over dough. Arrange ½ the pepperoni slices and ½ the sausage evenly over sauce. Top with 1 cup cheese. Repeat layers with remaining dough, sauce, pepperoni, sausage, and cheese.
4. Cover and cook on HIGH 1-½ hours. Uncover and let set 5 minutes. To serve, spoon this out and, if desired, top with additional sauce.

Did You Know?

Not all pizzas are created equally. Some have thin crusts, others thick ones...like this one. Which is your favorite?

Black Bean Enchiladas

Serves 5

- ¼ cup chopped onion
- ½ red bell pepper, chopped
- 1 (16-ounce) can black beans, drained, rinsed
- ½ cup frozen corn
- 2 teaspoons chili powder
- 1 teaspoon cumin
- ½ teaspoon salt
- 1-½ cups shredded Monterrey Jack cheese, divided
- 4 cups salsa
- 10 (6- to 8-inch) flour or corn tortillas

1. In a medium bowl, mix together onion, bell pepper, black beans, corn, chili powder, cumin, salt, and ½ cup cheese.
2. Pour 1 cup salsa into bottom of 6-quart or larger slow cooker and spread evenly.
3. Spoon about ⅓ cup black bean filling down center of each tortilla, roll them up, and place 5 in bottom of slow cooker. Spread 1 cup of salsa over this layer and sprinkle with ½ cup cheese. Place remaining enchiladas on top to create a second layer. Top with 1 cup salsa.
4. Cover and cook on LOW 3 hours. In the last 15 minutes of cooking, sprinkle remaining cheese over top and let melt. Serve enchiladas with remaining salsa.

Lighten it Up:

This is a great dish if you want to have a meatless dinner every once in a while. The best part is that the black beans are packed with protein. Also, as a way to lighten these up, you could use a reduced-fat cheese and whole wheat tortillas. Either way, muy bueno!

2-Minute Poached Salmon

Serves 4

4 (4-ounce) salmon fillets

Salt and pepper for sprinkling

4 lemon slices, plus more for garnish (optional)

4 sprigs fresh dill, plus more for garnish (optional)

2 tablespoons butter

1 cup water

½ cup white wine

1 Cut 4 pieces of aluminum foil into 6- x 6-inch pieces. Place a salmon fillet on each piece; sprinkle with salt and pepper. Top each with a lemon slice, a sprig of dill, and ½ tablespoon of butter. Seal each foil packet by folding ends securely.

2 In a 5-quart or larger pressure cooker, place a steamer insert or foil collar (see page xiii). Add water and white wine to pressure cooker, then place foil packets into cooker with two on the bottom and the others on top.

3 Securely lock lid and over high heat, bring to full pressure; reduce heat just enough to maintain pressure for 2 minutes. Perform a quick release.

4 Carefully remove and open packets. Serve with lemon and more fresh dill, if desired.

Did You Know?

Foil packet cooking is the perfect way to cook fish in a pressure cooker. It allows the fish to hold its shape, yet comes out moist and flavorful every time.

If using an electric pressure cooker prepare as directed above except:

- In step 3, set timer for 2 minutes.

For more details about how to use an electric pressure cooker, see pages xv-xvi.

Lemonade Fish Rollups

Serves 4

4 (4- to 5-ounce) mild white fish fillets

1 (.7-ounce) packet Italian dressing mix

1-½ cups lemonade

1 tablespoon cornstarch

2 tablespoons water

1 teaspoon lemon zest

⅛ teaspoon salt

1. Sprinkle both sides of each fillet with Italian dressing mix. Roll each fillet and secure with a toothpick or skewer.
2. Set a steamer insert (see page xiii) in the bottom of a 5-quart or larger pressure cooker. Pour lemonade in bottom. Place rollups on steamer insert.
3. Securely lock lid and over high heat, bring to full pressure; reduce heat just enough to maintain pressure for 2 minutes. Perform a quick release.
4. Remove fish to a platter and cover to keep warm. In a small bowl, whisk cornstarch and water. Over medium heat, heat liquid left in pressure cooker. Stir in cornstarch mixture and simmer 5 minutes, or until thickened. Add lemon zest and salt; drizzle over fish and serve.

Did You Know?

The combo of cornstarch and water that is used to thicken sauces is called a "slurry". It's a super quick way to turn pan drippings into a light sauce.

If using an electric pressure cooker prepare as directed above except:

- In step 3, set timer for 2 minutes.
- In step 4, simmer according to manufacturer's directions for your model.

For more details about how to use an electric pressure cooker, see pages xv-xvi.

Spinach and Shrimp Risotto

Serves 4

- 1 tablespoon butter
- 1 tablespoon olive oil
- 1 onion, chopped
- 1 stalk celery, chopped
- 1 clove garlic, chopped
- 1 cup Arborio rice
- 2 teaspoons oregano
- ⅛ teaspoon white pepper
- 2-½ cups chicken broth
- ¼ cup white wine
- 12 ounces medium shrimp (fresh or frozen and thawed, uncooked, peeled with tails removed)
- 2 cups fresh spinach, chopped
- ½ cup grated Parmesan cheese

1 In a 6-quart pressure cooker over medium heat, melt butter with oil. Add onion, celery, and garlic and sauté about 2 minutes, or until onions are tender. Add rice and stir. Sauté 1 more minute, then add oregano, pepper, broth, and wine. Bring to a simmer, and stir.

2 Securely lock lid and over high heat, bring to full pressure; reduce heat just enough to maintain pressure for 4 minutes. Perform a quick release.

3 Stir in shrimp and spinach and over low heat, simmer 3 to 4 minutes, or until shrimp turn pink. Stir in Parmesan cheese and serve.

Food for Thought:
This is the type of recipe where the pressure cooker really shines. You have dinner on the table in about 20 minutes and it tastes like you slaved over the stove all day. Really!

If using an electric pressure cooker prepare as directed above except:

- In step 1, sauté and simmer according to manufacturer's directions for your model.
- In step 2, set timer for 4 minutes.
- In step 3, simmer according to manufacturer's directions for your model.

For more details about how to use an electric pressure cooker, see pages xv-xvi.

Shrimp Alfredo

Serves 4

- 2 tablespoons olive oil
- ½ cup diced onion
- 8 ounces uncooked small shell pasta
- 2-½ cups chicken broth
- 1 tablespoon minced garlic
- 1 teaspoon Old Bay seasoning
- 12 ounces medium shrimp, (fresh or frozen and thawed, uncooked, peeled with tails left on)
- ½ cup heavy cream
- 1 cup grated Parmesan cheese
- 1 teaspoon all-purpose flour
- Salt and pepper to taste
- 1 tablespoon chopped fresh parsley

1. In a 6-quart or larger pressure cooker, heat oil on HIGH; add onion and sauté about 3 minutes, or until translucent. Add pasta, broth, garlic, and Old Bay seasoning; mix well.

2. Securely lock lid and over high heat, bring to full pressure; reduce heat just enough to maintain pressure for 3 minutes. Perform a quick release.

3. Add shrimp and over high heat, simmer for 2 minutes. Stir in heavy cream, Parmesan cheese, flour, salt, and pepper. Let simmer 2 to 3 more minutes, or until shrimp are pink. Stir in parsley and serve.

Food for Thought:
Have you ever tried buying Parmesan cheese that's sold as a chunk, and grated it yourself? Treat yourself some time, because the nutty flavor and the texture are out of this world.

If using an electric pressure cooker prepare as directed above except:

- In step 1, sauté according to manufacturer's directions for your model.
- In step 2, set timer for 3 minutes.
- In step 3, simmer according to manufacturer's directions for your model.

For more details about how to use an electric pressure cooker, see pages xv-xvi.

Cheeseburger Goulash

Serves 6

- 1 tablespoon vegetable oil
- 1 pound lean ground beef
- 1 small green bell pepper, diced
- 1 small yellow onion, diced
- 1 (8-ounce) package sliced mushrooms
- 1 cup beef broth
- 1 teaspoon garlic powder
- 3 cups uncooked elbow macaroni
- 1 (24-ounce) jar spaghetti sauce
- 1-½ cups shredded mozzarella cheese

1. In a 6-quart or larger pressure cooker, heat oil on HIGH until sizzling. Add beef and cook until browned. Add remaining ingredients except cheese. Do not stir.
2. Securely lock lid and over high heat, bring to full pressure; reduce heat just enough to maintain pressure for 5 minutes. Perform a quick release.
3. Stir well and top with cheese. Allow to melt 5 minutes, then serve.

Did You Know?

Here in the Test Kitchen we love our mashups, so when Patty said let's combine America's favorite sandwich with good old elbow macaroni, we jumped for joy.

If using an electric pressure cooker prepare as directed above except:

- In step 1, brown according to manufacturer's directions for your model.
- In step 2, set timer for 5 minutes.

For more details about how to use an electric pressure cooker, see pages xv-xvi.

Miracle Pasta Under Pressure

Serves 4

- 1 onion, thinly sliced
- 4 cloves garlic, thinly sliced
- 2 teaspoons dried oregano
- ½ teaspoon crushed red pepper flakes
- ½ teaspoon salt
- 3 cups chicken broth
- 12 ounces linguine, uncooked, broken in half
- 1 (28-ounce) can diced tomatoes
- 2 tablespoons olive oil
- 2 tablespoons chopped fresh basil
- Grated Parmesan cheese for sprinkling

1. In a 6-quart or larger pressure cooker add all ingredients, except basil and cheese, in order listed; stir gently.
2. Securely lock lid and over high heat, bring to full pressure; reduce heat just enough to maintain pressure for 5 minutes. Perform a quick release.
3. Stir in basil and sprinkle with Parmesan cheese before serving.

We bet you're looking at this recipe and saying "There's no way that this is going to work." Well, it does, and it's quite tasty. See, miracles do come true!

If using an electric pressure cooker prepare as directed above except:

- In step 2, set timer for 5 minutes.

For more details about how to use an electric pressure cooker, see pages xv-xvi.

Sensational Sidekicks

Steakhouse Onions

Serves 6

- 3 onions, peeled and cut in half horizontally
- 1 cup chicken broth
- 2 tablespoons olive oil
- 1 teaspoon chopped fresh rosemary
- ½ teaspoon salt
- ¼ teaspoon black pepper
- ¼ cup heavy cream
- 1 tablespoon all-purpose flour
- Ground nutmeg for sprinkling

1. Place onions cut side up in a 6-quart or larger oval slow cooker. Pour chicken broth over onions and drizzle with olive oil. Sprinkle with rosemary, salt, and pepper.
2. Cover and cook on HIGH 2 hours.
3. In a small bowl, combine heavy cream and flour; whisk until smooth. Pour mixture over onions and sprinkle with nutmeg.
4. Cover and cook an additional 45 minutes, or until sauce is thickened and onion tops are golden.

Food for Thought:

This recipe was inspired by those creamy baked onions we sometimes get at fancy steakhouses. And not only do they go with steak, they are just as fitting with roast pork, grilled chicken, or even a good old hamburger.

Old-Fashioned Sausage Stuffing

Serves 10

- 1-½ sticks butter
- ¾ cup chopped onion
- ¾ cup chopped celery
- 3 cups hot chicken broth
- 4 cups cubed herb-seasoned stuffing
- 4 cups crushed herb-seasoned stuffing
- 2 cups bulk pork sausage, cooked and crumbled

1. In a large skillet over high heat, melt butter. Add onion and celery, and cook 6 to 8 minutes, or until tender.
2. Meanwhile, in a large bowl, combine remaining ingredients. Add the cooked onions and celery, and toss gently to mix. Do not over mix. Place in a 5-quart or larger slow cooker.
3. Cook on LOW 3 to 3-½ hours, or until heated through and the edges are crispy. Serve immediately.

Cooking this in a slow cooker not only keeps it super moist, it frees up oven space which is super handy around the holidays.

Country Sliced Potatoes

Serves 8

- 2-½ pounds baking potatoes, thinly sliced (6 to 8 potatoes)
- 1 large onion, thinly sliced
- ¾ cup coarsely chopped crispy cooked bacon, divided
- 1 stick butter, melted
- 1-½ teaspoons salt
- ½ teaspoon black pepper

1. In a large bowl, combine potatoes, onion, ½ cup bacon, the butter, salt and pepper; toss gently. While tossing, separate potato slices that are stuck together so everything gets well coated. Arrange evenly in a 5-quart or larger slow cooker.
2. Cover and cook on LOW 7 to 8 hours or on HIGH 4 to 5 hours, or until fork-tender and the edges begin to brown. Gently stir halfway through cooking.
3. Sprinkle with remaining bacon and serve immediately.

Test Kitchen Mr. Food Hints & Tips

The best way to slice the potatoes nice and thin is either with a mandolin or a food processor with a slicing blade. That makes everything uniform. If you don't have either, no problem, just use a sharp knife and cut away.

Slow "Roasted" Country Corn

Serves 6

½ stick butter, melted
½ teaspoon salt
¼ teaspoon black pepper
1 tablespoon sugar
6 ears corn, shucked
½ cup water

1. Cut 6 pieces of aluminum foil, each about 8 inches long. In a small bowl combine butter, salt, pepper, and sugar.
2. Place each ear of corn on a piece of foil and evenly brush with butter mixture. Wrap foil around corn and seal the ends. Place wrapped corn in a 5-quart or larger slow cooker. Add water.
3. Cover and cook on LOW 4-½ to 5 hours or on HIGH 3 hours, or until tender. Carefully unwrap foil and serve immediately.

Food for Thought:
The slow cooking adds a rich, nutty flavor to the corn and brings out its natural sweetness. Plus, since the corn is already buttered and seasoned right out of the pot, it makes serving it so much easier.

North Carolina Corn Pudding

Serves 8

- 1 (8-ounce) package cream cheese, softened
- 2 eggs, beaten
- ½ cup sugar
- 2 cups frozen corn
- 1 (14.75-ounce) can cream-style corn
- 1 (8-½-ounce) package cornbread muffin mix
- ¾ cup milk
- 2 tablespoons butter, melted
- 1 teaspoon salt

1. Coat a 5-quart or larger slow cooker with cooking spray.
2. In a large bowl, mix together cream cheese, eggs, and sugar. Add remaining ingredients, mix well, and pour into slow cooker.
3. Cover and cook on LOW 5 to 6 hours or on HIGH 3 hours, or until center is set. Serve immediately.

Food for Thought:
Keep this recipe in mind around the holidays when your oven is full and the last thing you need is something else to keep an eye on. Having a slow cooker in your kitchen will be like having an extra pair of hands.

Chunky Cranberry Applesauce

Makes about 4 cups

- 3 pounds apples (6 to 9), peeled, cored, and cut into 1-½-inch chunks
- 1 cup fresh or frozen cranberries
- 1 cup apple juice or cider
- ⅓ cup sugar
- ⅛ teaspoon salt

1. In a 4-quart or larger slow cooker, combine all ingredients. Cover and cook on LOW about 4 hours, or until apples are very soft and begin to break up.

2. Mash apples and cranberries with a fork. Serve warm, at room temperature, or chilled.

Although this will work with almost any apple, we think this is best with Granny Smiths or other hearty baking apples. Oh, and feel free to make this as chunky or as smooth as you like!

Sunday Dinner Cauliflower

Serves 8

- 1 (10.5-ounce) can condensed Cheddar cheese soup
- ½ cup water
- 2-½ cups shredded Cheddar cheese
- 1 tablespoon Dijon mustard
- ½ teaspoon salt
- ¼ teaspoon black pepper
- 2 heads cauliflower, cut into large florets
- 4 slices bacon, cooked crispy and coarsely crumbled

1. In a large bowl, combine soup, water, cheese, mustard, salt, and pepper. Stir in the cauliflower and toss to coat. Pour into a 5-quart or larger slow cooker.

2. Cover and cook on LOW 4 to 5 hours, or until the cauliflower is fork-tender. Sprinkle with bacon and serve.

Food for Thought:

We got this recipe from a viewer who said her family served this every Sunday as part of their big dinner. She said she would put this on before going to church and when dinner time came, it was bubblin' hot and ready. Emily, thanks for sharing.

Boston Baked Beans

Serves 8

- 6 strips of bacon, diced
- 1 large onion, diced
- 1 (1-pound) bag dried navy beans, rinsed and drained
- 3-½ cups water
- 1 tablespoon vegetable oil
- ⅛ teaspoon ground cloves
- ½ teaspoon salt
- ¼ teaspoon black pepper
- ¾ cup ketchup
- ½ cup molasses
- ¾ cup brown sugar
- ¼ cup yellow mustard

1 In a 6-quart or larger pressure cooker over high heat, sauté bacon and onion about 5 minutes, or until bacon is nearly crisp. Add beans, water, oil, cloves, salt and pepper.

2 Securely lock lid and over high heat, bring to full pressure; reduce heat just enough to maintain pressure for 25 minutes. Perform a natural release.

3 Over medium heat, stir in remaining ingredients and let simmer 5 minutes. Add additional water, if necessary, to reach desired consistency.

If using an electric pressure cooker prepare as directed above except:

- In step 1, sauté according to manufacturer's directions for your model.
- In step 2, set timer for 25 minutes.
- In step 3, simmer according to manufacturer's directions for your model.

For more details about how to use an electric pressure cooker, see pages xv-xvi.

Cantina Black Beans

Serves 8

- 4 tablespoons olive oil, divided
- 1 (½-inch thick) slice deli ham, diced
- 1 onion, diced
- 3 cloves garlic, minced
- 1 bay leaf
- 1 (1-pound) bag dried black beans, rinsed and drained
- 6 cups water
- 2 teaspoons salt
- ½ teaspoon black pepper

1. In a 6-quart or larger pressure cooker over medium-high heat, add 3 tablespoons oil. Add ham and onion and sauté about 5 minutes, or until onion is translucent. Add garlic and bay leaf and continue to cook 1 minute. Stir in remaining ingredients.
2. Securely lock lid and over high heat, bring to full pressure; reduce heat just enough to maintain pressure for 25 minutes. Perform a natural release.
3. Remove bay leaf, discard, and stir well before serving.

If the beans are not as tender as you like, place the lid on loosely and simmer until tender.

If using an electric pressure cooker prepare as directed above except:

- In step 1, sauté according to manufacturer's directions for your model.
- In step 2, set timer for 25 minutes.

For more details about how to use an electric pressure cooker, see pages xv-xvi.

Tropical Sweet Potato Mash

Serves 8

- 1 (15-ounce) can pineapple chunks, undrained
- ¼ cup water
- 4 large sweet potatoes, peeled and cut into 2-inch chunks (about 3 pounds)
- 4 tablespoons butter
- ¼ cup brown sugar
- ½ teaspoon salt

1. Pour juice from pineapple and the water into a 6-quart or larger pressure cooker. Do not add pineapple yet. Place a steamer insert into the cooker (see page page xiii) and place the sweet potatoes and pineapple on top.

2. Securely lock lid and over high heat, bring to full pressure; reduce heat just enough to maintain pressure for 7 minutes. Perform a natural release.

3. Remove sweet potatoes and pineapple to a large mixing bowl. Add remaining ingredients and ¼ cup of the liquid from the pressure cooker, and beat with an electric mixer until smooth. Serve immediately.

Food for Thought:
When you are pressed for time, pull out your pressure cooker and go to town. Now you can have fork-tender sweet potatoes in about 10 minutes.

If using an electric pressure cooker prepare as directed above except:

- In step 2, set timer for 7 minutes.

For more details about how to use an electric pressure cooker, see pages xv-xvi.

Garlic Smashed Potatoes

Serves 8

3 pounds redskin potatoes, washed and cut into quarters
1-½ cups water
1 tablespoon kosher salt
6 cloves garlic
½ stick butter
2 tablespoons sour cream
1 teaspoon salt
¼ teaspoon black pepper

1. Place potatoes and water in a 5-quart or larger pressure cooker. Top with kosher salt and garlic cloves.
2. Securely lock lid and over high heat, bring to full pressure; reduce heat just enough to maintain pressure for 7 minutes. Perform a quick release.
3. Drain potatoes in a colander. Return potatoes to pressure cooker and cook over medium heat to cook off any excess water.
4. Transfer potatoes to a large bowl and add butter, sour cream, salt, and pepper. Beat with an electric mixer or mash with a potato masher to desired consistency.

Did You Know?
The reason we use whole cloves of garlic and kosher salt in this recipe is because they hold up better under pressure. The more coarse the grind of the spice, the more flavor.

If using an electric pressure cooker prepare as directed above except:

- In step 2, set timer for 7 minutes.
- In step 3, cook according to manufacturer's directions for your model.

For more details about how to use an electric pressure cooker, see pages xv-xvi.

PRESSURE COOKER

Maple Butter Acorn Squash

Serves 6

2 acorn squash
1 cup water
½ stick butter, melted
½ cup maple syrup
¼ teaspoon salt

1. On a cutting board, carefully cut each acorn squash in half. Using a spoon, remove the seeds and the stringy center. Place each piece cut-side down and cut into thirds.
2. In a 6-quart or larger pressure cooker, place a steamer basket (see page xiii). Place squash into the pressure cooker and add water.
3. Securely lock lid and over high heat, bring to full pressure; reduce heat just enough to maintain pressure for 6 minutes. Perform a quick release.
4. Cover a baking sheet with aluminum foil. Place squash on baking sheet skin-side down. Preheat the boiler. In a bowl, combine the remaining ingredients and brush half the sauce over the squash.
5. Broil 4 to 5 minutes, or until the glaze begins to caramelize. Remove from broiler, drizzle with remaining sauce, and serve.

If using an electric pressure cooker prepare as directed above except:

- In step 3, set timer for 6 minutes.

For more details about how to use an electric pressure cooker, see pages xv-xvi.

Grandma's Pickled Beets

Serves 12

- 6 medium beets
- 4 cups water, divided
- 1 onion, cut in half and thinly sliced
- ½ cup apple cider vinegar
- ½ cup sugar
- 1 teaspoon salt

Serving Suggestion:
These will last in the fridge for weeks in a tightly sealed jar. The reason we suggest storing these in glass is because the glass won't stain or absorb the odor from the beets and onion.

1. Trim the long root from the beet, but do not peel. (This will help the beet keep its color while cooking.) In a 6-quart or larger pressure cooker, place steamer insert (see page xiii). Add the beets and pour 3 cups water over the top.

2. Securely lock lid and over high heat, bring to full pressure; reduce heat just enough to maintain pressure for 24 minutes. Perform a natural release.

3. Remove beets to a baking sheet (so your counter won't get stained from the beet juice), trim ends with a knife, and peel off the skin. Cut beets into 1-inch chunks. Place in a bowl.

4. Add remaining water and remaining ingredients to pressure cooker. Over medium heat, bring to simmer and cook 2 to 3 minutes, or until the sugar dissolves. Remove from heat and pour over the beets. Let marinate at least 2 hours in the refrigerator before serving.

If using an electric pressure cooker prepare as directed above except:

- In step 2, set timer for 24 minutes.
- In step 4, simmer according to manufacturer's directions for your model.

For more details about how to use an electric pressure cooker, see pages xv-xvi.

Cinnamon-Kissed Carrots

Serves 6

- 1-½ pounds carrots
- 1 cup orange juice
- ¼ cup plus 1 tablespoon water, divided
- 1 cinnamon stick
- 3 tablespoons light brown sugar
- ½ teaspoon salt
- 1 teaspoon cornstarch

1. In a 5-quart or larger pressure cooker, place steamer insert (see page xiii). Cut each carrot in half lengthwise and then into 2-inch chunks, and place them on the insert. Pour orange juice and water over carrots; add cinnamon stick.

2. Securely lock lid and over high heat, bring to full pressure; reduce heat just enough to maintain pressure for 6 minutes. Perform a natural release. Remove carrots to a bowl and discard cinnamon stick. Remove steamer basket.

3. Over medium heat, bring the orange juice mixture in the pressure cooker to a simmer. Stir in brown sugar and salt. In a small bowl, whisk cornstarch and remaining water. Slowly whisk mixture into pressure cooker and let simmer until it thickens. Add the carrots back to the sauce until heat through. Serve immediately.

Adding a cinnamon stick to the water really infuses the carrots with lots of flavor. On top of that, your whole house will smell delicious.

If using an electric pressure cooker prepare as directed above except:

- In step 2, set timer for 6 minutes.
- In step 3, simmer according to manufacturer's directions for your model.

For more details about how to use an electric pressure cooker, see pages xv-xvi.

Blonde Mac & Cheese

Serves 8

- 2-½ cups uncooked elbow macaroni
- 3 cups water
- ½ teaspoon onion powder
- 2 tablespoons butter
- ¼ cup grated Parmesan cheese
- 8 ounces Muenster cheese, shredded
- 4 ounces cream cheese
- ½ teaspoon salt

1. In a 5-quart or larger pressure cooker, combine macaroni, water, onion powder, and butter.
2. Securely lock lid and over high heat, bring to full pressure; reduce heat just enough to maintain pressure for 2 minutes. Perform a quick release, and drain excess liquid..
3. Add remaining ingredients, stirring until cheese is melted and mixture is well combined. Serve immediately.

Howard Says:

"If your kids or grandkids like rotini, penne or shells better than elbows, no problem. The key to this recipe is all the cheesy goodness that coats each noodle. Have a ball."

If using an electric pressure cooker prepare as directed above except:

- In step 2, set timer for 1 minute.

For more details about how to use an electric pressure cooker, see pages xv-xvi.

Super-Fast Mushroom Risotto

Serves 6

- 2 tablespoons olive oil
- 2 tablespoons butter
- 3 cloves garlic, minced
- 1 onion, chopped
- 2 cups Arborio rice
- 2 tablespoons white wine (optional)
- 4 cups chicken broth
- 8 ounces sliced mushrooms
- 2 tablespoons Parmesan cheese
- ½ teaspoon salt
- ¼ teaspoon pepper

1. In a 6-quart or larger pressure cooker over medium-high heat, add oil and butter. Add garlic and onion and sauté until translucent. Add rice and continue to cook until the rice begins to brown. Stir in wine, if desired, and cook about 1 minute, or until wine has evaporated. Add broth and mushrooms; mix well.

2. Securely lock lid and over high heat, bring to full pressure; reduce heat just enough to maintain pressure for 9 minutes. Perform a quick release.

3. Stir in Parmesan cheese, salt, and pepper. Serve immediately.

Did You Know?

The consistency of risotto should be wet and sticky. If this is too wet after pressure is reduced, cook it with the lid off until it reaches desired consistency. If you think it is a bit too dry, or after letting it sit, you may want to stir in some chicken broth or water and reheat slowly.

If using an electric pressure cooker prepare as directed above except:

- In step 1, sauté according to manufacturer's directions for your model.
- In step 2, set timer for 9 minutes.

For more details about how to use an electric pressure cooker, see pages xv-xvi.

To Satisfy Every Sweet Tooth

Fudgy S'more Cake

Serves 6

- 1 (15.25-ounce) package devil's food cake mix, batter prepared according to package directions
- 1-½ cups semisweet chocolate chips, divided
- 1-½ cups coarsely chopped graham crackers
- 1-½ cups miniature marshmallows

1. Coat a 2- to 3-½ quart slow cooker with cooking spray. Pour batter into slow cooker; mix in 1 cup chocolate chips and the graham crackers.
2. Cover and cook on HIGH 2 to 2-½ hours, or until toothpick inserted in center comes out clean.
3. Turn off slow cooker and sprinkle marshmallows and remaining chocolate chips over top of cake. Cover and let sit 10 minutes, then spoon warm cake into dessert dishes and serve.

A little tip when making this, make sure you add the marshmallows and remaining chocolate chips at the very end like the recipe says, so they melt slowly, yet still retain some of their shape. The results are...yum, yum, yum!

The World's Moistest Carrot Cake

Serves 8

- 1 cup shredded carrot, plus extra for garnish
- 1 cup chopped walnuts
- 1 (21.45-ounce) package carrot cake mix, batter prepared according to package directions
- 1 (16-ounce) container cream cheese icing

1. Coat a 5-quart slow cooker with cooking spray.
2. Stir 1 cup carrots and the walnuts into prepared batter until well combined. Pour into slow cooker. Place a double layer of paper towels over top of slow cooker and place lid on. (See page viii.)
3. Cook on HIGH 1-½ to 2 hours, or until a toothpick inserted in center comes out clean. Remove cooking insert to a wire rack to let cool 15 minutes. Run a knife around the edge, and place serving plate upside-down over cooking insert; carefully invert and remove cake from pan.
4. Frost with cream cheese icing and sprinkle with remaining shredded carrot.

Food for Thought:
Worried that baking a cake for this long will result in a dry texture? No worries, because the slow cooker keeps almost all of its steam trapped inside, so cakes always come out super-moist. Yes, that's the secret to their moistness.

Pineapple Upside-Down Cake

Serves 8

- 1 cup packed brown sugar
- ½ stick butter, melted
- 1 (20-ounce) can pineapple slices in juice, drained with juice reserved
- 8 maraschino cherries without stems, drained
- 1 (15.25-ounce) package yellow cake mix

1. Coat a 6-quart slow cooker with cooking spray.
2. In a small bowl, mix brown sugar and butter; spread evenly in bottom of slow cooker. Arrange pineapple slices over brown sugar mixture, cutting as needed to fit in one layer. Place cherry in center of each slice and around slices, as needed.
3. Add enough water to reserved pineapple juice to measure 1 cup. Make cake batter as directed on package, substituting pineapple juice mixture for water. Pour batter over pineapple and cherries. Place a double layer of paper towels over top of slow cooker and cover with lid. (See page viii.)
4. Cook on HIGH 2 to 2-1/2 hours, or until toothpick inserted in center comes out clean. Turn off slow cooker; uncover. Remove cooking insert from cooker to cooling rack. Let cool 10 minutes.
5. Run a knife around the edge, and place serving plate upside-down over cooking insert; carefully invert and remove cake from pan.

Test Kitchen Mr. Food Hints & Tips

Before turning this out onto the platter, just make sure that the platter is larger than the mouth of your cooking insert. If not...you'll have quite the mess. Trust us!

Glazed Lemon Poppy Cake

Serves 8

- 2 cups all-purpose flour
- ¼ cup poppy seeds
- 1 tablespoon baking powder
- ½ teaspoon salt
- 1 cup sugar
- 3 eggs
- ½ cup vegetable oil
- ½ cup plain Greek yogurt
- ¼ cup milk
- 1 teaspoon grated lemon zest
- ¼ cup fresh lemon juice
- 1 teaspoon vanilla extract

LEMON GLAZE

- 2 cups confectioners' sugar
- ½ teaspoon grated lemon zest
- 3 tablespoons lemon juice

1. In a large bowl, combine flour, poppy seeds, baking powder, and salt; set aside.

2. In a medium bowl, whisk together sugar, eggs, oil, yogurt, milk, lemon zest, lemon juice, and vanilla until sugar dissolves. Add sugar mixture all at once to flour mixture. Stir just until combined. (Mixture will be slightly lumpy.) Spoon batter into a 5-quart slow cooker that has been coated with cooking spray. Place a double layer of paper towels across opening and place lid on.

3. Cover and cook on HIGH 2 hours, or until toothpick inserted in center comes out clean. Turn off slow cooker. Remove cooking insert to a wire rack and cool 10 to 15 minutes. Run a knife around the edge, and place serving plate upside-down over cooking insert; carefully invert and remove cake from pan. Cool completely.

4. Meanwhile, in a medium bowl, whisk confectioners' sugar, lemon zest, and lemon juice until smooth. Drizzle over cake.

Put your glaze into a resealable plastic bag and cut just a very small piece off the corner to glaze the cake. You can then pipe stripes going one way, then the other for a more decorative effect.

Peanut Butter Cup Cake

Serves 10

- 1 (15-ounce) package gluten free devil's food cake mix
- 1 cup chocolate chips
- 1 (8-ounce) package cream cheese, softened
- 1 stick butter, softened
- 1 cup peanut butter
- 2 cups confectioners' sugar
- 1 teaspoon vanilla extract
- ½ cup mini peanut butter cups, cut in half

1. Prepare cake batter according to package directions; stir in chocolate chips. Pour batter into a 4-quart slow cooker coated with cooking spray. Place paper towels over opening and place lid on.
2. Cook on HIGH 1-¾ to 2 hours, or until toothpick inserted in center comes out clean. Remove cooking insert from slow cooker to a wire rack. Let cool 15 minutes. Run a knife around the edge, and place serving plate upside-down over cooking insert; carefully invert and remove cake from pan.
3. In a large bowl, make frosting by mixing cream cheese, butter, and peanut butter until thoroughly combined. Mix in confectioners' sugar and vanilla until smooth.
4. Slice cake in half horizontally to make 2 layers. Place one layer on platter and frost. Place second layer over frosted layer and frost top and sides. Sprinkle with peanut butter candies and serve, or refrigerate until ready to serve.

Food for Thought:

This cake is amazing and no one would ever know that it is gluten free. We dare you to challenge your family with this cake to see if they can tell.

Apple Cinnamon Cobbler

Serves 8

- 8 Fuji apples, peeled and cut into ½-inch slices
- ¼ cup granulated sugar
- 2 tablespoons plus ¼ cup all-purpose flour, divided
- 2 tablespoons butter, melted
- ¼ cup cinnamon candies (like Red Hots)
- ¾ cup quick-cooking oatmeal
- ¼ cup light brown sugar
- ½ stick butter, cut into small pieces

1. Coat a 4- to 5-quart slow cooker with cooking spray.
2. In a large bowl, gently toss apples, granulated sugar, 2 tablespoons flour, the butter, and cinnamon candies. Place mixture in slow cooker.
3. In a medium bowl, combine oatmeal, brown sugar, remaining flour, and the butter; mix until crumbly. Sprinkle over apples.
4. Cover and cook on LOW 3 hours, or until apples are tender and topping is golden.

Howard Says:

"Yes, this is good by itself, but to take it over the top, how about serving it with a big scoop of vanilla ice cream and a drizzle of caramel sauce? My mouth waters just thinking about how good this was."

Strawberry Rhubarb Heaven

Serves 6

- 1 (16-ounce) package frozen whole or halved strawberries
- 1 (16-ounce) package frozen rhubarb
- 1 cup plus 2 tablespoons sugar, divided
- 6 tablespoons (3/4 stick) butter, softened, divided
- 1 tablespoon cornstarch
- 1 teaspoon vanilla extract
- 1 cup all-purpose flour
- 1 egg
- 1/4 teaspoon salt

1. Coat a 4- to 5-quart slow cooker with cooking spray.
2. In a large bowl, combine strawberries, rhubarb, 1 cup sugar, 2 tablespoons butter, the cornstarch, and vanilla; mix well then pour into slow cooker.
3. In a medium bowl, combine flour, egg, salt, remaining sugar, and remaining butter; mix until crumbly, then sprinkle over fruit mixture.
4. Cover and cook on HIGH 2 to 2-1/2 hours, or until strawberries are bubbling and topping is set. Serve warm.

Did You Know?

It may look like there's a lot of sugar in this recipe, but trust us, this recipe needs it as the rhubarb is very tart. Of course, if you want to cut it back a bit you can, but if you do, get ready to pucker up.

Your Very Own Cheesecakes

Serves 4

CRUST

¾ cup graham crackers

3 tablespoons sugar

5 tablespoons melted butter

FILLING

1 (8-ounce) package cream cheese, softened

½ cup sugar

1 egg

½ teaspoon vanilla extract

½ cup sour cream

1. In a bowl, combine all ingredients for the crust; mix well. Evenly divide mixture into 4 (1-cup) ramekins. Press down mixture firmly to create a crust.

2. In another bowl, beat together cream cheese and sugar until smooth. Add egg, vanilla, and sour cream and mix well. Evenly spoon mixture into ramekins.

3. Place 1 cup of water in the bottom a 6-quart or larger slow cooker. Place ramekins into the slow cooker.

4. Cover and cook on LOW 2 hours, or until center is set.

5. Carefully remove from slow cooker and cool on counter before refrigerating at least 2 hours, to firm up before serving.

Serving Suggestion:

How about topping these with some fresh berries, sliced kiwi, or whatever you have on hand? After all, it's your very own!

Cookies & Cream Cheesecake Loaf

Serves 8

10 chocolate sandwich cookies, crushed

3 tablespoons butter, melted

2 (8-ounce) packages cream cheese, softened

½ cup sugar

2 eggs

1 teaspoon vanilla extract

6 chocolate sandwich cookies, coarsely chopped

1. In a small bowl, combine the crushed cookies and butter. Pour into an 8- x 4-inch loaf pan and press down firmly to form a crust. (Make sure the pan fits in your slow cooker before preparing.)

2. In a large bowl, with an electric mixer, beat the cream cheese and sugar until smooth. Add eggs and vanilla and mix until well combined. Do not over mix. Gently stir in the chopped cookies. Pour the into loaf pan. Pour 1 cup of water into a 5-quart or larger slow cooker and place loaf pan into cooker.

3. Cover and cook on LOW 2-¾ to 3 hours, or until the center is set. Remove loaf pan and let cool 1 hour on wire rack before refrigerating.

4. Refrigerate at least 3 hours before serving. Cut into one-inch slices and enjoy.

Baking a cheesecake in a slow cooker is a fool-proof way for it to come out perfect every time, since it cooks it nice and slow. That means no cracks in the top and lots of creaminess in every bite. Now that's our idea of the perfect dessert!

Peanut Butter Chocolate Crunchies

Makes 64 pieces

- 2 cups mini marshmallows
- 1 (8-ounce) package mini peanut butter cups
- 1 cup chocolate chips
- ½ cup peanut butter
- ⅓ cup evaporated milk
- 1 cup chopped peanuts
- 1 cup potato sticks
- 1 cup coarsely crushed pretzels
- 1 cup confectioners' sugar

1. Place marshmallows, peanut butter cups, chocolate chips, peanut butter, and evaporated milk in a 2-½ quart slow cooker; stir until mixed.
2. Cover and cook on HIGH 30 to 45 minutes, or until mixture is melted and smooth, stirring occasionally.
3. Coat an 8-inch square baking dish with cooking spray.
4. Add peanuts, potato sticks, pretzels, and sugar to chocolate peanut butter mixture; stir until well combined. Pour mixture into baking dish.
5. Chill at least 1 hour, then cut into squares and serve.

Food for Thought:

Slow cookers are great to make candy or to melt chocolate in since the heat is low and the chocolate doesn't scorch. Wow, just another way to use your slow cooker like never before.

Almond Bread Pudding

Serves 10

- 3 cups plus 1 tablespoon milk, divided
- ¾ cup granulated sugar
- 3 eggs
- 2 teaspoons almond extract
- ¼ teaspoon salt
- 1 (16-ounce) loaf stale Hawaiian sweet bread, cut into 1-inch cubes
- ¼ cup sliced almonds
- ¾ cup confectioners' sugar

1. In a large bowl, whisk together 3 cups milk, the granulated sugar, eggs, almond extract, and salt. Add bread cubes and stir to coat with liquid. Cover and refrigerate 30 minutes.
2. Pour mixture into a 5-quart or larger slow cooker. Sprinkle with almonds.
3. Cover and cook on LOW 4 to 4-½ hours, or until a knife inserted in center comes out clean.
4. In a bowl, whisk confectioners' sugar and remaining milk until smooth. Drizzle over bread pudding and serve warm.

Serving Suggestion:

To make this fancy schmancy, rather than serving it from the slow cooker, remove the cooking insert to a wire rack and let it cool 15 minutes. Run a knife around the edge, and place a plate upside-down over cooking insert; carefully invert and remove bread pudding from pan. It will be hot, so put on those pot holders. Then place a platter over it and invert right side up, drizzle with glaze, and serve.

Meltaway Turtle Surprise

Serves 6

- 1-½ cups pancake and baking mix
- 1 cup sugar, divided
- ½ cup unsweetened baking cocoa
- ½ cup milk
- ¾ cup caramel topping, divided
- 1-½ cups hot water
- ½ cup chopped pecans

1. Coat a 3-quart slow cooker with cooking spray.
2. In a large bowl, combine baking mix, ½ cup sugar, and the cocoa. Stir in milk and ½ cup caramel topping until well blended. Pour into slow cooker and pour hot water over top. (Do not stir.) Sprinkle with remaining sugar.
3. Cover and cook on LOW 3 to 3-¼ hours, or until top springs back when touched lightly. (Center will still be soft.) Turn off slow cooker; let stand uncovered 20 minutes to cool slightly. Serve warm, garnished with remaining caramel topping and pecans.

Serving Suggestion:

We like to balance out all the sweetness by topping this with some lightly whipped cream. Spoon it on and get ready for lots of mm, mm, mmm!

Raspberry Poached Pears

Serves 4

½ cup warm water
¼ cup sugar
2 cups frozen raspberries
4 pears, peeled
1 tablespoon cornstarch
2 tablespoons water

1. In a 4- to 5-quart slow cooker, add warm water and sugar, and stir until dissolved. Stir in raspberries. Place pears, standing upright, on top of raspberry mixture.
2. Cover and cook on LOW 3-½ to 4 hours, or until fork-tender. Spoon sauce over pears half-way through cooking.
3. Remove pears to a platter. Turn slow cooker to HIGH. In a small bowl, whisk together the cornstarch and water and slowly whisk into raspberry sauce. Heat about 5 minutes, or until sauce slightly thickens.
4. Serve raspberry sauce over pears, either warm or chilled.

Since most pears are not flat on the bottom, we discovered that if you trim about ¼-inch off the bottom, they will stand up nice and straight. It's all these little tricks that help you cook like a pro.

"Baked" Apples

Serves 5

- 5 large apples
- ¼ cup oats
- ¼ cup brown sugar
- 1 teaspoon cinnamon
- 5 tablespoons butter
- ½ cup apple juice or water

1. Core apples, leaving a 1-inch diameter hole; remove seeds.
2. In a bowl, combine oats, brown sugar, and cinnamon. Evenly fill each apple with mixture. Place in a 6-quart or larger slow cooker. Top each with a tablespoon of butter. Pour juice around apples (not over).
3. Cook on HIGH 3 hours, or until apples are fork-tender. Remove from slow cooker, spoon juices over apples, and serve.

Food for Thought:

You won't need an air freshener while this dessert is cooking. It'll fill your whole house with the scent of grandma baking an apple pie. Oh, those memories!

SLOW COOKER

Can-Do Strawberry Bread

Serves 12

- 2 cups frozen strawberries, thawed and mashed
- 1 cup sugar
- ½ cup vegetable oil
- 2 to 3 drops red food coloring
- 2 eggs
- 1-¼ cups plus 1 tablespoon self-rising flour, divided
- ½ cup chopped pecans
- 2 cups water

1. Using 3 empty 15- to 16-ounce vegetable cans, remove labels, wash, dry, and coat with cooking spray; set aside.
2. In a large bowl, with an electric mixer on low speed, mix strawberries, sugar, oil, food coloring, and eggs, until well mixed. Add 1-¼ cups flour and continue mixing until well combined.
3. In a small bowl, toss pecans with remaining flour then stir into batter. Pour batter into cans, filling only ⅔ full.
4. Pour water into 5-quart or larger slow cooker. Stand cans upright in cooker and cook on HIGH 2 to 2-½ hours, or until toothpick inserted in center of each comes out clean. Remove cans to a wire rack and cool 10 to 15 minutes. Run a knife around the edge of each, and carefully remove loaves.

Pumpkin Patch Bread

Serves 10

- 1-¼ cups whole wheat flour
- 1 teaspoon baking soda
- ½ teaspoon cinnamon
- ¼ teaspoon nutmeg
- ¼ teaspoon cloves
- ¼ teaspoon salt
- 1 stick butter, softened
- ¾ cup packed brown sugar
- 1 egg
- 1 (15-ounce) can pumpkin (not pumpkin pie filling)
- 1 teaspoon vanilla extract

1. Coat a 5-quart slow cooker with cooking spray.
2. In a large bowl, combine flour, baking soda, cinnamon, nutmeg, cloves, and salt.
3. In a medium bowl, combine butter, brown sugar, egg, pumpkin, and vanilla. Add to flour mixture and mix well. Place batter in slow cooker. Place a double layer of paper towels across opening (see page viii) and cover.
4. Cook on LOW 4-½ hours, or until toothpick inserted in center comes out clean. Remove cooking insert to a cooling rack and cool 10 to 15 minutes. Run a knife around the edge, and place serving plate upside-down over cooking insert; carefully invert and remove from pan.

When baking in a slow cooker, it's a good idea to remove the cooking insert halfway through and turn it 180 degrees. This way, whatever you're baking browns evenly on all sides.

Chocolate Chip Banana Bread

Serves 8

- 3 tablespoons canola oil
- ½ cup sugar
- 2 eggs, beaten
- ⅓ cup buttermilk
- 3 ripe bananas, mashed
- 1-½ cups all-purpose flour
- 1 teaspoon baking soda
- ¼ teaspoon salt
- ½ cup chocolate chips
- ¼ cup chopped walnuts (optional)

1. Coat an 8- x 4-inch loaf pan with cooking spray. (Be sure it fits into a 5- to 6-quart slow cooker.)

2. In a large bowl, combine oil, sugar, eggs, buttermilk, and bananas; beat until thoroughly mixed. Beat in flour, baking soda, and salt just until blended. Stir in chocolate chips and nuts, if desired. Pour batter into loaf pan and place in slow cooker. Place a double layer of paper towels over top of cooker and place lid on. (See page viii).

3. Cook on HIGH 2 to 2-½ hours, or until a toothpick inserted in center comes out clean.Remove pan to a wire rack to cool. Slice and serve.

If your bananas aren't ripe enough to make banana bread, stick them on a parchment-lined baking sheet and then into a 300° oven for about 30 minutes. They'll turn black, be soft to the touch, and perfect for your bread. Also, if you want, you can always bake this directly in a 4-quart slow cooker instead of in the loaf pan, yup...right in the cooking insert.

Gooey Pecan Sticky Buns

Serves 8

PECAN TOPPING

½ stick butter, melted

¼ cup light brown sugar

½ teaspoon cinnamon

½ cup chopped pecans

BUNS

¼ cup light brown sugar

½ teaspoon cinnamon

2 tablespoons butter, melted

1 (12-ounce) package refrigerated biscuits (10 biscuits)

1. Line the bottom and sides of a 5- to 6-quart slow cooker with aluminum foil.

2. In a small bowl, combine all the pecan topping ingredients; mix well. Place mixture on the foil in the slow cooker and spread evenly. (This will become the topping after this bakes.)

3. To make the buns, in a bowl, combine brown sugar and cinnamon. After separating the biscuits, dip both sides of each biscuit into butter, then into brown sugar mixture. Place on top of the pecan mixture in the slow cooker.

4. Cover and cook on LOW 4 hours, or until puffed and golden. Immediately remove the sticky buns by lifting out the foil and inverting onto a serving platter. Slowly peel back the foil. Be careful, this will be very hot. Let cool slightly before serving warm.

In this recipe, it's easier to use regular aluminum foil rather than heavy-duty because the heavy-duty is harder to mold to the inside of the slow cooker.

Peach Foster Ice Cream Crepes

PRESSURE COOKER

Serves 10

- 5 (9-inch) refrigerated ready-to-use crepes
- 1-½ quarts vanilla ice cream
- 6 peaches, sliced
- 1 cup peach nectar
- ½ stick butter
- ¾ cup light brown sugar
- 1 tablespoon cornstarch
- 2 tablespoons water
- 1-½ cups frozen whipped topping, thawed

1. Lay crepes on the counter and evenly divide ice cream down center of each; gently roll crepes around ice cream. Let sit for a moment so ice cream softens slightly and can be formed into one long roll. Place on a platter and freeze immediately.

2. In a 6-quart or larger pressure cooker, combine peaches, peach nectar, butter, and sugar.

3. Securely lock lid and over high heat, bring to full pressure; reduce heat just enough to maintain pressure 3 minutes. Perform a quick release. Using a slotted spoon, gently remove peaches to a bowl, leaving sauce in pressure cooker.

4. In a small bowl, combine cornstarch and water; whisk into pressure cooker. Simmer over medium-high heat until thickened, then return peaches to sauce and stir gently.

5. Remove crepes from freezer, cut in half, top with warm peaches and sauce, garnish with whipped topping, and serve immediately.

If using an electric pressure cooker prepare as directed above except:

- In step 3, set timer for 3 minutes.
- In step 4, simmer according to manufacturer's directions for your model.

For more details about how to use an electric pressure cooker, see pages xv-xvi.

Decadent Chocolate Custard

PRESSURE COOKER

Serves 3

- ½ cup heavy cream
- ¼ cup milk
- ¼ cup sugar
- ½ teaspoon vanilla extract
- ¾ cup semi-sweet chocolate chips
- 3 egg yolks, lightly beaten
- 2 cups water

1. In a saucepan over medium-low heat, combine heavy cream, milk, sugar, and vanilla; stir. Remove from heat then add chocolate chips and stir until melted. Whisk in egg yolks. Pour mixture into 3 (½-cup) ramekins and cover each with foil.
2. In a 6-quart or larger pressure cooker, place a steamer insert or trivet. (See page xiii.) Add water to pressure cooker. Place ramekins on insert.
3. Securely lock lid and over high heat, bring to full pressure; reduce heat just enough to maintain pressure 7 minutes. Perform a quick release.
4. Remove ramekins from the pressure cooker and uncover. Let cool 20 minutes on the counter, then refrigerate at least 2 hour before serving.

Serving Suggestion:

If you are a chocolate lover, fasten your seatbelt and get ready for one of the most decadent desserts you've ever indulged in. If you want, you can always add a dollop of whipped cream and some fresh berries to cut the richness.

If using an electric pressure cooker prepare as directed above except:

- In step 3, set timer for 7 minutes.

For more details about how to use an electric pressure cooker, see pages xv-xvi.

Diner-Style Rice Pudding

Serves 6

- 1 cup long grain white rice
- 2-½ cups water
- 2 tablespoons butter
- ¼ cup salt
- 1-½ cups milk
- ½ cup sugar
- ¼ cup raisins
- 1 teaspoon vanilla extract

1. In a 5-quart or larger pressure cooker, combine rice, water, butter, and salt.
2. Securely lock lid and over medium-high heat, bring to full pressure; reduce heat just enough to maintain pressure for 8 minutes. Perform a quick release.
3. Remove lid and stir in milk; mix well, making sure to get any rice that may have stuck to the bottom. Stir in sugar and raisins.
4. Simmer over low heat about 5 minutes, or until mixture begins to thicken. Stir in vanilla and serve warm or chill until ready to serve.

We found it's better to add the sugar and milk after it's pressure cooked. That way it won't scorch the bottom and it still comes out nice and creamy!

If using an electric pressure cooker prepare as directed above except:

- In step 2, set timer for 8 minutes.
- In step 4, simmer according to manufacturer's directions for your model.

For more details about how to use an electric pressure cooker, see pages xv-xvi.

Shortcut Crème Brulee

Serves 4

3 egg yolks

7 tablespoons sugar, divided

1 cup heavy cream

2 teaspoons vanilla extract

2 cups water

1. In a medium bowl, combine egg yolks and 3 tablespoons sugar; whisk until sugar is dissolved. Add heavy cream and vanilla, and whisk just enough to mix well. Do not overmix. Pour mixture into 4 (½-cup) ramekins and cover each tightly with foil.

2. In a 6-quart or larger pressure cooker, place a steamer insert or trivet. (See page xiii.) Add the water to the cooker then place 2 ramekins onto insert.

3. Securely lock lid and over high heat, bring to full pressure; reduce heat just enough to maintain pressure 5 minutes. Perform a quick release. Remove ramekins and cool, uncovered, 20 minutes. Meanwhile, repeat with remaining ramekins.

4. Once cooled, cover and refrigerate 2 to 4 hours, or until chilled.

5. Right before serving, preheat broiler. Sprinkle with remaining sugar, and place under broiler 3 to 5 minutes, or until sugar is caramelized.

When broiling, make sure you keep a close eye on these because they can go from golden to overdone in seconds.

If using an electric pressure cooker prepare as directed above except:

- In step 3, set timer for 5 minutes.

For more details about how to use an electric pressure cooker, see pages xv-xvi.

Chocolate Chip Croissant Bread Pudding

Serves 3

- 1 egg
- ¾ cup heavy cream
- 2 tablespoons sugar
- ½ teaspoon vanilla extract
- 4 mini or 2 regular-size frozen croissants, cut into 1-inch chunks
- 2 tablespoons chocolate chips

1. Place a steamer insert or foil collar (see page xiii) in bottom of a 6-quart or larger pressure cooker.
2. In a large bowl, whisk egg, heavy cream, sugar, and vanilla. Stir in croissants and chocolate chips until evenly coated. Evenly distribute between 3 (¾-cup) ramekins. Place ramekins carefully on steamer insert.
3. Securely lock lid and over high heat, bring to full pressure; reduce heat just enough to maintain pressure 3 minutes. Perform a quick release. Allow to cool slightly and serve.

Check out page xv to learn more about cooking in a crock. It's really easy!

If using an electric pressure cooker prepare as directed above except:

- In step 3, set timer for 3 minutes.

For more details about how to use an electric pressure cooker, see pages xv-xvi.

Index

Index